Production Code Basics
For Movie Still Collectors

By
Ed and Susan Poole

A Publication by
MovieStillID.com &
LearnAboutMoviePosters.com
of the
Learn About Network, L.L.C.

Production Code Basics for Movie Still Collectors

Published by:
Ed and Susan Poole
P. O. Box 3181
Harvey, LA 70059
edp@LearnAboutMoviePosters.com

© 2014 by Ed and Susan Poole
All Rights Reserved.

No part of this publication may be reproduced, stored in a database, or transmitted in any form, or by any means, electronic, mechanical, photocopying, recording, or otherwise, without prior written permission
of the Authors/Publishers.

The Authors/Publishers have used their best efforts in preparing this publication. Authors/Publishers make no representation or warranties with respect to the accuracy or completeness of the contents of this publication and specifically disclaim any implied warranties of merchantability or fitness for any particular purpose and shall in no event be liable for any loss of profit or any other commercial damage, including but not limited to special, incidental, consequential, or other damages.

ADDITIONAL COPIES:

Additional copies of this publication are available through the authors:

Ed Poole
P. O. Box 3181
Harvey, LA 70059
(504) 298-LAMP
Email: edp@LearnAboutMoviePosters.com

or online at www.MovieStillID.com or
www.LearnAboutMoviePosters.com

TABLE OF CONTENTS

Acknowledgements i

From the Authors ii

Introduction to Film Production Stills iii

Chapter 1: The Cinema Begins 1

Chapter 2: From the Executive Level 11

Chapter 3: Production Process 19

Chapter 4: Publicity Department 35

Chapter 5: Advertising Department 57

Chapter 6: Special Photographer 65

Chapter 7: Outside Major Studio Framework 75

Chapter 8: Common Problems With All Studios ... 87

Chapter 9: Individual Studios 105

Chapter 10: Tools for Identifying Unknown
            Movie Stills 129

ACKNOWLEDGEMENTS

In 2007, on our trip to Cinevent, we asked dealers at the convention what areas needed research and documentation. The overwhelming response was "production codes," as nothing was available. This book, as a companion guide to our *Movie Still Identification Book*, is our response to those dealers' request.

Special thanks have to go to four special people for their help with this book. Those are Barry Gilliam, Rudy Franchi, Richard Finegan and Gene Arnold. Without them, this book would not be possible.

We wanted to limit the advertisements in this book to just our regular sponsors to honor them. So when you see an advertisement, please remember that these wonderful sponsors care enough about the research, documentation and preservation of film accessories to sponsor us.

The support of the LAMP sponsors and dealers found throughout this book allows us the capability to present information, such as this book and our *Movie Still Identification Book,* to help YOU. Please support them whenever possible. We have a list of these wonderful sponsors on the last page of this book.

FROM THE AUTHORS

As the only film accessory researchers in the world, we are on a quest to preserve, document, and compile as much information as possible to keep film accessories (movie posters, stills, pressbooks, and props) from experiencing the same fate as early films have in the United States.

The declaration that 80-90% of all silent films made in the U.S., plus 50% of all U.S. films produced before 1951 (when they created safety film), **are already lost forever** makes the preservation of the film accessories as the remaining historical documents of this social media even more imperative.

But what good is it to preserve these historical movie stills when you can't identify them.

We have spent thousands of hours in the research and compilation of over 50,000 production codes to help with that identification.

Now we hope this companion book on *Production Code Basics For Movie Still Collectors* will help show how to utilize those codes to assist in the identification.

INTRODUCTION TO FILM PRODUCTION STILLS

Although the motion picture camera is credited with the creation of the worldwide cinema, still photography was basically the backbone of the industry. The use of still photography was, and still is, an integral part of the process of producing, distributing and marketing a film.

Starting in 1912 and expanding to all major studios during the teens, production, distribution and marketing stills were controlled by an accounting process called "Production Codes."

To understand the importance of production codes, we must first understand movie stills. And to understand movie stills we need to understand why they were made and how they were used.

Movie stills fall into many categories including: promotional, publicity, paparazzi, production, portrait, photographer, celebrity, autographed, and even amateur, etc.

In this book, we are addressing the production, portrait, shorts and TV stills that have identifiable markings that were placed by the distribution and production companies.

The first step in this journey is to understand how and why production codes came about. We will then look at the process that was used and how and why production codes were applied by various studios and distributors.

> *Please note that the following information is based on the "general" process followed by major studios for decades before the digital revolution. Each studio, however, would vary these procedures to meet their own specific needs. We will cover some of these variations later in the book.*

CHAPTER 1

THE CINEMA BEGINS

To understand the use of production codes, you really need to look at HOW and WHY it was started. To do that you need to go all the way back to the very beginning.

French Film Domination

Contrary to popular belief, the United States was not always the dominant country in filming. In the beginning of the cinema, it was the French.

The Lumiere Brothers began their marketing in France around the same time as it began in the United States. The early films consisted of scenes of everyday occurrences such as waves crashing on shore, trains arriving and departing, factory workers at lunch, etc.

The public soon tired of these actuals, and the popularity of films began to wane. Fortunately for the movie industry, two French film pioneers took the fledging cinema into a whole new direction.

France's Alice Guy worked as the secretary to film producer Leon Gaumont. During her private time, Guy borrowed Gaumont's camera to shoot stories on film for her garden club. These movies were so popular that they led to the development of narrative film.

Frenchman George Melies would take the concept of storytelling on film one step further when he introduced the public to special effects such as stop motion, fade in and out (and even the first nudie movies), etc.

While Thomas Edison was spending the majority of his energy trying to stop other filmmakers in the United States, the Lumiere Brothers used the 1897 Belgian World's Fair to reach out to all major countries around the world. *(See our **Learn About International Movie Posters** book for more details).*

Soon afterwards, the Pathe Brothers bought out the Lumiere Brothers and created the first mass production of films. Pathe established seven different production companies each taking a week to produce a film. Their output was seven films a week equating to one new film released EVERY DAY.

It was stated in court at the famous Motion Picture Patents Company ("MPPC") trials that in 1906, Pathe ALONE had an estimated 60% share of the U.S. market. And it was estimated that by 1908, the French film companies controlled 70-80% of the WORLD market.

By 1907, independent production companies began popping up all over the United States. So much so that in March of 1907, a new magazine, Moving Picture World, was launched.

The first issue was primarily about the Edison – Biograph court battles. There were 12,000 copies of MPW's first issue printed, which sold out immediately. (All of the early MPW magazines are available online in the advance member section of GlobalCinemaResearch.org.)

By 1908, Edison realized had he lost the battle fighting alone. He tried another tactic by creating the Motion Picture Patents Company, better known as "The Trust."

The goal of this coalition of all the major American film companies was to maintain control and form a front against the French film invasion. While it worked temporarily, it backfired and ignited the rebellion of the independents. This, however, is a topic for another day.

Distribution of Early Films

During the formative years of the cinema, films were made by the production company and then SOLD by the FOOT. This was fine for travelling showmen who exhibited to changing audiences, but horrible for stationary theaters that relied on repeat business.

As old films piled up at the theaters, film exchanges were introduced. These exchanges would rent or exchange films so that theaters could swap out movies, getting something new without shelling out large amounts of money each week for new films. These film exchanges were extremely popular.

During the pre-studio era (before the fall of the Edison Trust in 1915), movie releases were generally handled in one of two ways—either by road show or states rights.

Road show meant that the film would travel around the country stopping at specific theaters for special showings, one after the other. For larger productions, several teams would travel around the country at the same time.

States Rights meant that the production company would sell the rights to distribute their film in a particular territory to a distributor or exchange.

Both roadshow and states rights created spotty distribution across the country and were extremely taxing on the production company. But BOTH methods also proved ineffective for wide-scale national feature distribution.

Below is an ad from a new independent exchange in Philadelphia in 1911 that was buying the output of films from Imp, Thanhouser, Reliance and Bison.

ATTENTION, EXHIBITORS
A New Independent Exchange for Philadelphia

1. We wish to announce to the trade that we have opened an Independent film exchange at 23 N. 9th Street, Philadelphia, Pa., and that we offer exhibitors of the city and surrounding territory an
EXCEPTIONAL UP-TO-DATE FILM SERVICE

2. We are buying the output of the Motion Picture Distributing and Sales Co., and we can guarantee for every week the entire output of the Imp, Thanhouser, Reliance, Bison and American manufacturers.

3. We have absolutely no dead stock on hand. All our films are new. Think of the great advantage of dealing with a new exchange, to be able to secure clean, new films of almost any subject desired.

4. We have a triplicate checking system and we furnish you with a typewritten list of your daily program so you can file same and at all times have a record of your past exhibitions.

5. We can book you on a definite date from date of release.

6. We furnish posters with every reel, also a ten-foot banner for the feature reel.

7. We invite you to our offices to inspect our system and our examining department. We thoroughly examine and put in first-class condition every reel before leaving our place and therefore assure you of no broken sprocket holes which tend to wrench your machine and spoil your show.

8. Come and see us and let us quote you our price, or write, wire or 'phone.

Exhibitors Film Service Co., 23 North Ninth St. Philadelphia, Pa.

Many of the larger production companies began looking for ways to merge their output and create national distribution.

National Film Distribution

At the same time, one of Edison film exchange managers, W. W. Hodkinson, came up with a better way to handle distribution.

Hodkinson was Special Representative to the General Film Company representing the Motion Picture Patents Company in Salt Lake City and Los Angeles. He envisioned a nationwide distribution structure that would make states rights obsolete, and provide profit-sharing with producers to encourage filmmakers to concentrate on higher quality films that would yield higher box office.

Under the Hodkinson system, the distributor would provide a cash advance to an independent producer to cover the costs of producing each feature film. The distributor then received the exclusive rights to the finished movie, using a network of exchanges to control distribution and marketing, and even offering to pay for the producer's film prints and advertising.

Hodkinson kept 35 percent of the box office as a distribution fee, and gave the rest of the profits back to the producer. Hodkinson discovered that by financing film producers, the distributor was guaranteed a steady stream of high-class pictures without ever having to operate a film camera. In addition, the producers made more money than they would under the states rights system without any of the marketing headaches.

In April 1911, as a test, Hodkinson began to implement his system by reorganizing the San Francisco area for General Film. The test market generated fantastic results. In 1912 however, Hodkinson encountered resistance from the Trust who refused to enact his new procedure in other regions.

In November 1912, Hodkinson made two comparative charts predicting, in one chart what the future of the film industry and General Film would be if his methods were adopted nationally; and the collapse of General Film if they were not. He traveled to New York for the presentation, but his system was rejected by the Patents Company members who told him to undo his successful San Francisco reforms. Hodkinson refused which caused him to be released.

During this trip to New York, Hodkinson established ties with some of the important independent studios including Adolph Zukor, who was then struggling under the states rights method. Zukor was the kind of producer who would benefit greatly by this new distribution procedure.

Hodkinson formed the Progressive Pictures Company, a west coast-based operation that distributed films for a number of independent production companies like the Famous Players Film Company and the Jesse L. Lasky Feature Play Company.

He decided to expand his west coast business into a national organization in early 1914, but discovered another east coast company with the same name as his own Progressive Pictures. When he went to New

York in 1914, he changed his company's name to Paramount Pictures, Inc. on May 8, 1914.

Hodkinson immediately had all the independent producers such as Zukor and Lasky sign five-year distribution contracts to assure availability for going nationwide.

Though the producers were far better off than they were under states rights, they soon started resenting the amount of profits they shared with Hodkinson. And even though Zukor himself was once an independent producer on the losing end of an unfavorable distribution deal, he seemed to harbor no sympathy for the next generation of independents who struggled as he had before. So Zukor devised a plan involving his friend Lasky that would turn the tables on Hodkinson.

Only one year into his five-year contract—and desperately wanting out—Zukor surprisingly renegotiated a new 25-year deal with Paramount on March 1, 1915. By May, Zukor and Lasky had sold a 51 percent interest in their production companies to Paramount Pictures. This made Zukor subordinate to Hodkinson's Paramount, but it also made Zukor and Lasky cash-rich. They opened up an extended line of credit that allowed them to secretly accumulate Paramount stock.

Zukor and Lasky together acquired a majority of the capital stock of Paramount Pictures, Inc. They then took control of Paramount and OUSTED Hodkinson. New directors were elected, followed by the forced resignation of Hodkinson and his treasurer Raymond Pawley on June 13, 1916.

Zukor appointed his own president Hiram Abrams as the new head of Paramount. On July 19, 1916, Zukor and Lasky merged their companies with Paramount, and created the Famous Players-Lasky Corporation, a $12.5 million producer-distributor—the largest film company at the time.

The Hodkinson distribution system proved so advantageous for all involved that, with slight modifications, it has remained in full practice in the U.S. to this day.

With this new model of national distribution in place, numerous national distributors began forming. BUT, another major change was also already underway.

International Change

During this time, World War I broke out in Europe, crippling and then collapsing the film industry in France and England. Pathe, Melies, and Gaumont all moved their international headquarters to the United States to try to avoid as much damage as possible. The European film industry lost their studios, management, actors and equipment which left a huge void in the international market.

Countries around the world were screaming for quality films for entertainment. With the European film industry in shambles and almost non-existent, the U.S. film industry began gearing up for the increase and takeover of the international market. BUT, with this overwhelming demand came a need to streamline the process, giving more control to management to enable more production by a larger number of production companies.

The drastic expansion in film production also caused numerous major advancements in filming equipment and techniques. New systems and procedures were enacted, such as scripting and closer budgeting. All these new procedures created an interlocking chain of command with the executives more in control of all the different steps. Let's look at some of the changes from an executive level and then work our way through the production process.

~~~~~~~~~

DO YOU HAVE POSTERS YOU WANT TO SELL?

THERE IS NO AUCTIONEER OF VINTAGE MOVIE PAPER WHO HAS LOWER FEES OR WHO DELIVERS CONSISTENTLY HIGHER PRICES THAN EMOVIEPOSTER.COM, AND WE ARE THE ONLY AUCTIONEERS WHO CAN TAKE ALL OF YOUR MOVIE PAPER!

EMOVIEPOSTER.COM
P.O. BOX 874
306 WASHINGTON AVE.
WEST PLAINS, MO 65775
WWW.EMOVIEPOSTER.COM
417-256-9616 · MAIL@EMOVIEPOSTER.COM

Movie Poster Frames
Direct from Studio Supplier

Specializing in framing your collectibles since 1984

Made to order custom frames
At Wholesale Prices
~ Delivered to your door ~

www.hollywoodposterframes.com
(800) 463-2994

9260 Deering Ave
Chatsworth, CA 91311

Open to public:
Thur-Fri: 10-5 p.m.
Sat: 9-2 p.m.

CHAPTER 2

FROM THE EXECUTIVE LEVEL

Let's start at the top and work our way down. Executives at the major studios were monitoring multitudes of films, so they didn't want all the details. Studio management only wanted to know basic information such as what was being filmed, the film's director, any major changes or modifications, and when filming was completed.

Shown below is an Executive Production Board from 1918. This board showed the names of different directors and the progress of their work. At a moment's glance it may be told how many actors are at work, how many scenes completed, and whether they are in the studio or out doing exteriors.

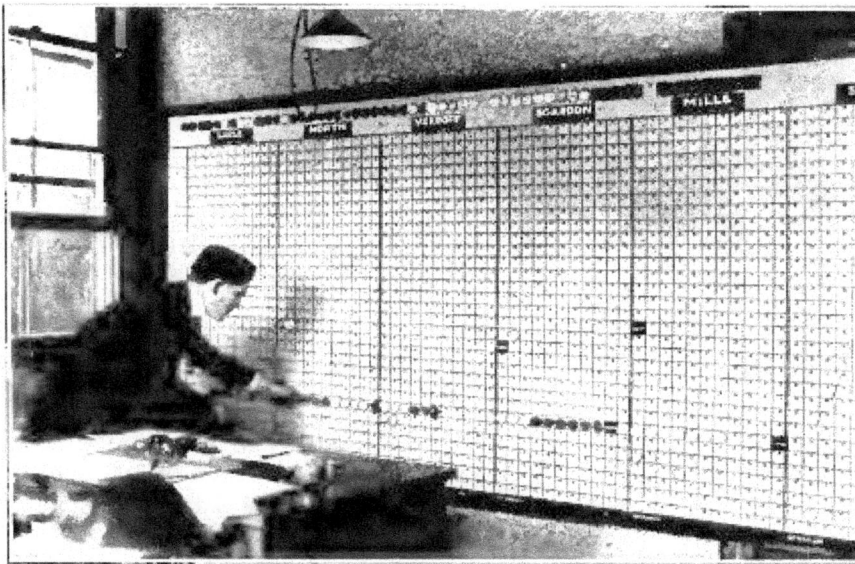

Some executives wanted a system to keep track of the basics that could be occasionally updated. A production NUMBER/CODE was created to follow through the process (because quite often titles and/or directors would change).

Again we want to pick on Paramount as all records seem to indicate they were the most aggressive and most likely the ones that actually started the use of production codes.

We want to show you a VERY RARE look at one of the systems used by Paramount to control their projects - Route Cards. Never heard of them, you say... yes, these are that hard to find.

From the late teens until the 1970s, a simple Route Card was issued showing what projects were in production by the production number, title and director. This simple card let executives see the number assigned, the title, if the title changed, the director, if the director changed, and when the production was completed. The entry would then drop off of all of the subsequent cards. This meant filming was completed and the film moved to the editing process.

We were able to study these cards in one binder of a two-binder set. We reviewed Volume 2, which covered the years 1943-1967. We have not yet been able to acquire Volume 1 to study. But the samples from Volume 2 show how their system worked.

Examples of these Route Cards follow. The actual cards are printed on colored card stock, each in a different color which made them easier to discern.

Paramount Pictures

ROUTE CARD No. 5
August 2, 1943

- 1356 Lady In The Dark — Lesser
- 1357 Riding High — Marshall
- 1361 The Story of Dr. Wassell — DeMille
- 1362 The Uninvited — Allen
- 1363 The Hour Before The Dawn — Tuttle
- 1364 And The Angels Sing — Marshall
- 1365 Henry Aldrich's Little Secret — Bennett
- 1366 Frenchman's Creek — Leisen
- 1367 Hail The Conquering Hero — Sturges
- 1368 Standing Room Only — Lanfield
- 1369 Ministry of Fear — Lang
- 1370 Going My Way — McCarey
- 1371 Henry Aldrich's Code Of Honor — Bennett
- 1372
- 1380 Dr. Wassell — Bacon-DeMille

ROUTE CARD No. 6
October 12, 1943

- 1356 Lady In The Dark — Lesser
- 1361 The Story of Dr. Wassell — DeMille
- 1362 The Hour Before The Dawn — Tuttle
- 1364 And The Angels Sing — Marshall
- 1366 Frenchman's Creek — Leisen
- 1367 Hail The Conquering Hero — Sturges
- 1368 Standing Room Only — Lanfield
- 1370 Ministry of Fear — Lang
- 1320 Going My Way — McCarey
- 1371 Henry Aldrich — Boy Scout — Bennett
- 1372 Our Hearts Were Young And Gay — Allen
- 1373 The Man In Half Moon Street — Murphy
- 1374 Rainbow Island — Tuttle
- 1375 Double Indemnity — Wilder
- 1376 Wear I Come Back — Sandrich
- 1377

ROUTE CARD No. 7
November 12, 1943

- 1354 — The Dark — Leisen
- 1361 The Story of Dr. Wassell — DeMille
- 1365 Frenchman's Creek — Leisen
- 1367 Hail The Conquering Hero — Sturges
- 1368 Standing Room Only — Lanfield
- 1369 Ministry of Fear — Lang
- 1370 Going My Way — McCarey
- 1371 Henry Aldrich — Boy Scout — Bennett
- 1372 Our Hearts Were Young And Gay — Allen
- 1373 The Man In Half Moon Street — Murphy
- 1374 Rainbow Island — Murphy
- 1375 Double Indemnity — Wilder
- 1376 I Love A Soldier — Sandrich
- 1377 Tomorrow's Harvest — Borzage
- 1378 The Hitler Gang — Farrow
- 1379 Incendiary Blonde — Marshall
- 1380 The Great —
-

ROUTE CARD No. 2
March 17, 1944

- 1366 Frenchman's Creek — Leisen
- 1367 Hail The Conquering Hero — Sturges
- 1374 Rainbow Island — Murphy
- 1376 I Love A Soldier — Sandrich
- 1377 Til We Meet Again — Borzage
- 1378 The Hitler Gang — Farrow
- 1379 Incendiary Blonde — Marshall
- 1382 Road To Utopia — Walker
- 1383 And Now Tomorrow — Pichel
- 1384 Bring On The Girls — Lanfield
- 1385 Practically Yours — Leisen
- 1386
- 1387
- 1388
- 1389
- 1390
- 1391

ROUTE CARD No. 3
May 11, 1944

- 1366 Frenchman's Creek — Leisen
- 1367 Hail The Conquering Hero — Sturges
- 1374 Rainbow Island — Murphy
- 1376 I Love A Soldier — Sandrich
- 1377 Til We Meet Again — Borzage
- 1379 Incendiary Blonde — Marshall
- 1382 Road To Utopia — Walker
- 1383 And Now Tomorrow — Pichel
- 1384 Bring On The Girls — Lanfield
- 1385 Practically Yours — Leisen
- 1386 Masters He Says — Marshall
- 1387 Two Years Before The Mast
- 1388 Here Come The Waves — Sandrich
- 1389 Fear — Allen
- 1390

- 13 -

These cards were kept in a ring binder. The ones we have on file were issued about every two months before and during World War II, but went to monthly as production picked up after WWII.

Here is a closer look at a portion of a page:

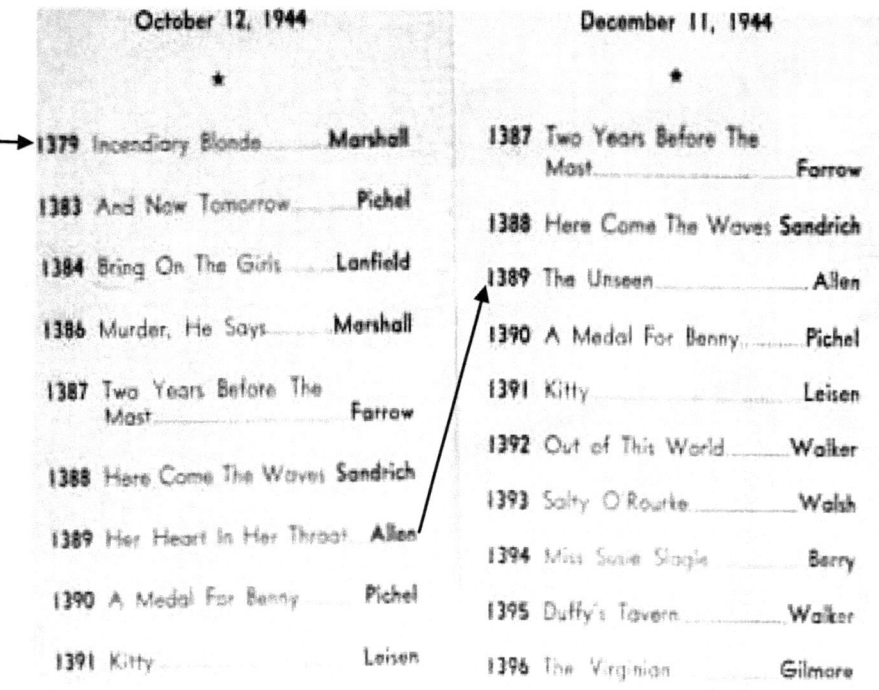

Notice the first one on the October sheet is #1379 – *Incendiary Blonde* – (director) Marshall. By the December card – it's gone. It was finished with filming and sent to editing. Notice down the line to #1389 – *Her Heart in Her Throat* (director) Allen. By December the title had been changed to *The Unseen*.

Let's look at another sample. The image on the next page shows three of the cards for May, June and July 1948:

11441 The Great Gatsby — Nugent	11442 Tatlock Millions — Mayan	11442 Tatlock Millions — [illegible]
11442 Tatlock Millions — Haydn	11443 Sorrowful Jones — Lanfield	11443 Sorrowful Jones — [illegible]
11443 Sorrowful Jones — Lanfield	11444 The Accused — Dieterle	• 11444 The Accused — Dieterle
11444 The Accused — Dieterle	11445 Dark Circle — Farrow	• 11445 Dark Circle — Farrow
11445 Dark Circle — Farrow	11446 Lady from Lariat Loop — Marshall	• 11446 Lady from Lariat Loop — Marshall
11446	11447 Streets of Loredo — Fenton	• 11447 Streets of Loredo — Fenton
11447	11448	- 11448 One Woman — Allen
11448	29022 Big Sister Blues — Ganzer	- 11449 Samson and Delilah — DeMille
29021 Tropical Masquerade — Ganzer	29023 Catalina Interlude — Ganzer	• 11450 A Mask for Lucretia — Leisen
29022 Big Sister Blues — Ganzer	29024	29022 Big Sister Blues — Ganzer
29023	10009 Sorry, Wrong Number — Litvak	29023 Catalina Interlude — Ganzer
29024	10010	29024
10009 Sorry, Wrong Number — Litvak	10011	• 10009 Sorry, Wrong Number — Litvak
10010	10012	- 10052 The Heiress — Wyler
	10052 The Heiress — Wyler	11513 Samson and Delilah (Morocco) (2nd Unit) — Jester
	11513 Samson and Delilah (2nd Unit) — DeMille	• 11514 Samson and Delilah (Studio) (3rd Unit) — Jennings
		• 11515 Samson and Delilah (Miniature) (4th Unit) — Jennings

On the June card (middle), the entry on the bottom reads: 11513 – *Samson and Delilah* (2nd Unit) (dir.) DeMille. Notice on the July card where the new number 11449 shows as the production code for *Samson and Delilah* with DeMille as the director.

The bottom of the July card reads: 11513 – *Samson and Delilah* (2nd Unit in Morrocco) with Jester as director; 11514 – *Samson and Delilah* (3rd Unit in Studio) with Jennings as director; and 11515 – *Samson and Delilah* (4th Unit - Miniature) Jennings over that as well. **These are temporary UNIT codes**. Once the filming was complete, temporary codes were eliminated and the primary number used.

Let's look at one more sample of two cards from May and June of 1962.

```
10380  It's Only Money . . . Tashlin          10381  Paris When It Sizzles . Quine

10381  Together in Paris . . . Quine          10382  Hud Bannon . . . . . . Ritt

10382  Hud . . . . . . . . . . Ritt          10383  Papa's Delicate
                                                     Delicate Condition . . Marshall
10383  . . . . . . . . . . . . .
                                              10384  . . . . . . . . . . . . . . . .
11543  My Six Loves . . . . Champion
                                              11543  My Six Loves . . . . Champion
31200 thru 31249 Gunsmoke/TV Series
                                              31200 thru 31249 Gunsmoke/TV Series
31150 thru 31199
    Have Gun - Will Travel/TV Series          31150 thru 31199
                                                  Have Gun - Will Travel/TV Series
31400 thru 31449 Bonanza/TV Series
                                              31400 thru 31449 Bonanza/TV Series
31300 thru 31349
    Pete and Gladys/TV Series . . . .         31300 thru 31349
                                                  Pete and Gladys/TV Series . . . .
```

Code #10381 has a name change from *Together in Paris* to become *Paris When It Sizzles*. Code 10383 starts out as *Pap's Delicate Delicate Condition*.

Also note that these cards show how TV series codes were listed in blocks. By this time, TV had become a major part of production as well and was integrated into the system.

Each TV episode had its own production code number. Notice that they would allocate a block of 50 numbers at a time. When they finished that block of 50, if the show was going to continue, they would allocate another block of 50 until the show was cancelled. And while the Route Cards only cover the series, we have been hard at work trying to break down each episode as well and fill those titles in.

~~~~~~~~~~

- ORIGINAL VINTAGE MOVIE POSTERS
- RARE FILM POSTERS BOUGHT AND SOLD
- LINENBACKING AND RESTORATION SERVICES
- EXPERT CUSTOM FRAMING

L'IMAGERIE ART GALLERY
In Business Since 1973

www.limageriegallery.com

PHONE: 818-762-8488   FAX: 818-762-8499   EMAIL: limageriegallery@gmail.com

10555 Victory Boulevard - North Hollywood, CA 91606
Tuesday through Saturday from 11:30 to 6:00

Ewbank's
Take a look at our auctions

www.ewbankauctions.co.uk

CHAPTER 3

PRODUCTION PROCESS

Still photography was an integral part of a movie's production process. It started BEFORE the actual filming and was going on simultaneously DURING the filming process until the film was completed.

This was one of the expanded control steps discussed earlier AND most important to our topic of discussion.

Still Photography

Each major studio normally had a **Unit Photographer** on staff for general photography purposes. In addition, particularly on larger productions, additional photographers were sometimes brought in for either overflow purposes or special assignments.

Secondary or Color Photographers were sometimes used for major productions, such as one photographer taking black & white and one taking color shots.

Also, on some major productions, **Special Assignment Photographers** were hired by the studios at the request of certain actors or publications. We will cover these in Chapter 6.

Unit Photographer

The images taken by the unit photographer or overflow photographer were developed daily and distributed to various departments for specific purposes.

The following outlines his work and the departments utilizing his stills. Each area will be addressed in detail in the following pages.

- Pre-Production
  - Casting
  - Hair, Makeup and Costume
- Production
  - Scene Continuity
  - Filming
- Publicity
  - Key Set Creation
  - Production Code Assignment
  - Exclusives
  - Portraits
- Advertising
  - Creation of Posters
  - Creation of Lobby Cards
  - Creation of Advertising Clips
  - Press Use - Studio/National Screen Service
  - New York Newspaper Set

Color Photographer

In early days and on smaller productions, the color photographer was also the unit photographer effectively pulling double duty.

For larger productions, it was common for a second photographer to be used on the set just to produce the color stills. This really increased in the 1960's when magazines and major publications started demanding more color.

These color stills were handled exactly the same as the standard black and white stills EXCEPT that they were a separate operation with different personnel. This operation was called the "Color Desk."

While this book focuses on production codes, the ultimate objective is to help identify that unknown movie still. You will probably run into all of these types and many times, just knowing the production code is not enough.

Like a detective, you have to continuously look for clues, so the more you understand the process, the more clues you will spot to help clear up more of those on-the-line questionable stills.

Let's follow the above outline through the different departments. We will be placing more emphasis on the areas that pertain more to production codes and all will become clear.

Pre-Production

The first stills taken on a film were normally shot long before filming actually began. They were incorporated into the initial planning and development of the project.

Basically, this means that THESE stills are NOT what this book is about as they did not utilize production codes.

These particular photographs were used in a variety of ways, including storyboarding, administrative decision-making, and conceptual artwork for early advertising campaigns. They also took wardrobe tests, hair and makeup tests and publicity tests.

A lot of times the original release still had a snipe or writing on the back to give the details. But again, this book is not about identifying "original" or any other type of authentication. We are assuming that there is NOTHING on the back and what you see on the front is what-you-get.

Some of these pre-production stills were used as "casting stills" as they featured photos of a "proposed" cast (as sometimes they would change before the actual production began).

For example, the image on the following page features a casting still showing Elizabeth Taylor in costume for the role of Lygia in the film *Quo Vadis*. But, by the time filming started, she was replaced by Deborah Kerr.

This casting still is identified by the black informational board in the lower left. It reads: "Elizabeth Taylor as Lygia, Costume 5-7 Quarry Costume."

The following two images are casting stills featuring Ann Sheridan as "Randy" in the film *Kings Row*. These examples demonstrate the inconsistency in the way studios marked, or didn't mark, their pre-production stills, even within the same film. For example, the still below was NOT marked.

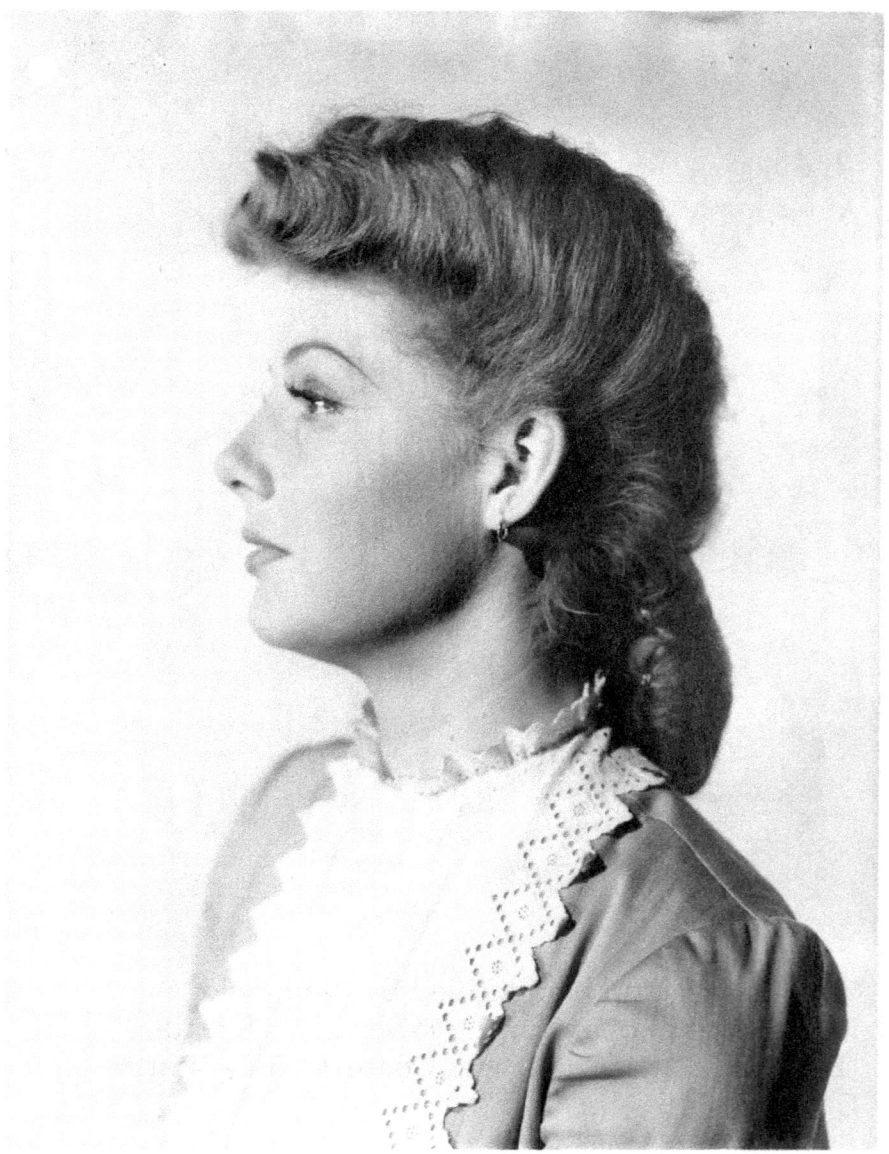

Unlike the still on the preceding page, this still is clearly marked.

NOTICE: both of these stills have 3 punch holes going down the left side. These holes will be covered in the next chapter.

Some stills have NO identifying markings, while others show just minimal information.

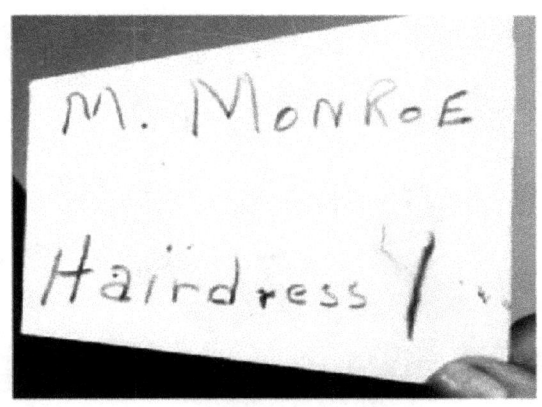

For example, the still on the preceding page shows only a hand holding a piece of scrap paper identifying Marilyn Monroe in a hairdress test. (Image above) We have NO CLUE what film this is from as there is just not enough information to cross reference.

When you are dealing with pre-production stills, you have inconsistent markings, usually very little information and no assurance that the actor was even in the film. Sometimes you can luck out and get a cool inside shot even when the title isn't shown. The image on the next page is an example of this.

The still features a young beautiful Elizabeth Taylor. While there is no title on this wardrobe still, the top line on the board identifies "Prod. 1315." Production Code 1315 was for the MGM film *National Velvet*.

The words "Training Pie" apparently refer to a working title since the horse in the film was named Pie. (Production codes will be discussed in more detail in Chapter 4).

(And yes, you can also see that Elizabeth Taylor's name was misspelled - Elisabeth Taylor).

Production

Once filming began on a film project, the unit photographer had several responsibilities. Here are just some of the duties of a movie set's unit photographer.

Scene Continuity

The unit photographer took photographs throughout the course of day's film shoot. These were used for a number of reasons. Some of these shots were used specifically for "scene continuity."

At the end of a day's film shoot, these scene continuity stills were used by the director and his production staff to make sure that each subsequent day's scene layout and props would match exactly with the prior day's scene.

This was a very important aspect of the unit photographer's job. These shots were essential to avoid filming mishaps such as appearing and disappearing salt shakers, curtains changing color, tables and chairs placed in different locations, etc.

These stills were marked and numbered in a WIDE variety of ways, but normally done together in a batch at the end of the day. Not all of these photographs would have the informational clapboard.

The still shown on the following page features a scene continuity shot from the 1946 RKO film, *It's a Wonderful Life*, starring James Stewart and Donna Reed.

Again, these are for your understanding and not part of the standard production code process.

Filming

During the production, the unit photographer was responsible for capturing thousands of still shots of the production. The photographer would stand next to a movie camera operator and take photographs that would appear almost identical to specific scenes in the film.

Some of the shots would offer a completely different angle than the motion picture camera and some of the shots would be behind the scenes with actors and directors or special set up for publicity shots.

At the end of the day, the motion picture film went one direction and the still camera film went a different direction, each to a completely different process.

After the production still shots were taken each day, the photographer would take the rolls of film negatives and place each role on a "contact sheet."

These contact sheets were created by laying the negatives on a piece of printing paper and exposing them to light to create a set of mini prints the same as the film frames.

The advantage to using a contact sheet was that all of the film negatives, generally around 36 images, could be viewed at one time with a "ring" or magnifying glass.

The negatives and contact sheets were then sent to the publicity department for review to pick out the best images to use for publicity.

The image below shows a typical contact sheet.

~~~~~~~~~~

FRENCH MOVIE POSTER

THOUSANDS OF ORIGINAL FRENCH MOVIE POSTERS FROM 1960'S TO NOW DAYS

contact@frecnhmovieposter.com
www.frenchmovieposter.com

There are 25,000 posters databased and available at www.movieart.com. Inquire to posters@movieart.com. We sell posters to collectors, designers and institutions worldwide. Our staff is friendly. We answer questions.

Selling posters since 1979.

IVPDA
international vintage
POSTER
dealers association

KIRBY McDANIEL
MOVIEART

kinoart.net

ORIGINAL MOVIE POSTERS AND LOBBY CARDS

12,000 SELECTED VINTAGE INTERNATIONAL POSTERS AVAILABLE

**WOLFGANG JAHN
SULZBURGSTR. 126
50937 COLOGNE
GERMANY
+49 221 1698728**

VINTAGE MOVIE POSTERS

WHEN YOU'RE READY TO SELL YOUR POSTERS, YOU'LL BE GLAD YOU CALLED US!

Every year Heritage Auctions holds three Signature® Movie Poster Auctions in March, July and November.

How can you be sure the offer to purchase your poster or poster collection is the absolute maximum? At Heritage our goal is to present each and every one of your items to the largest number of qualified buyers in the world. Why sell outright to a single buyer when our auction platform will bring multiple buyers to compete against each other? When the time comes to sell your treasures, call us; we'll be happy to give you a free appraisal.

Take a look at these examples and see for yourself how we realize more money for our movie poster consignors than all other auction firms combined!

The Black Cat (Universal, 1934)
One Sheet (27" X 41") Style B
Realized $334,600
November 2009

The Bride of Frankenstein (Universal, 1935)
One Sheet (27" X 41") Style D
Realized $334,600
November 2007

Flying Down to Rio (RKO, 1933)
One Sheet (27" X 41")
Realized: $239,000
November 2008

To consign to an upcoming auction, contact:

GREY SMITH
Director, Movie Poster Auctions
214-409-1367
GreyS@HA.com

Always accepting quality consignments in 38 categories.
Immediate cash advances available up to $50 million.

Free catalog and *The Collector's Handbook* ($65 value) for new clients. Please submit auction invoices of $1000+ in this category, from any source. Include your contact information and mail to Heritage, fax 214-409-1425, email catalogorders@HA.com, or call 866-835-3243. For more details, go to HA.com/FCO.

Annual Sales Exceed $900 Million | 850,000+ Online Bidder-Members
3500 Maple Ave. | Dallas, TX 75219 | 877-HERITAGE (437-4824) | HA.com
DALLAS | NEW YORK | BEVERLY HILLS | SAN FRANCISCO | HOUSTON | PARIS | GENEVA

THE WORLD'S LARGEST COLLECTIBLES AUCTIONEER
HERITAGE AUCTIONS HA.com

Licensed Auctioneer Andrea Voss: TX 16406. Buyer's Premium 19.5%. See HA.com for details.
HERITAGE Reg. U.S. Pat & TM Off.

32300

CHAPTER 4

PUBLICITY DEPARTMENT

The Publicity Department was, among other things, responsible for generating early publicity about a film, including providing information to magazines and publications. This is also the point where production code numbers were assigned.

The publicity department would review the contact sheets and create a "key set." From this "key set," images were selected for specific purposes, and provided to magazines and publications. **THESE** are some of the main stills that are targeted in this book for identification.

Key Set Creation

After a review by the publicity department, the better images were chosen to become part of a key set. The selected images were marked with the **assigned production number** and the individual still number. The stills were then printed and placed into the key set binder.

The rejected images were skipped over and **left unnumbered.** The negatives and contact sheets were then filed. These could be pulled and numbered at a later date if someone wanted something different.

By the end of the shooting, this key set would normally consist of hundreds of the better still shots to be used in a variety of ways by the publicity department. They were kept in large bound books that could be used at any time for reference. Here is a sample:

The key book on the preceding page was for the Paramount film *Dead On Arrival*, which was the working title. It was renamed *Girl in 419* as you can see written on the label and tag. It also shows the production code (937).

Shown below is a great shot of Wild Bill Elliott with Little Beaver (young Bobby Blake).

Notice that this still has two punch holes at the top. Sometimes stills would be placed on extended photo paper or a backing like this one, and sometimes the holes were punched directly into the still.

A lot of studios would then mark them on the back like this:

THIS IS A KEY SET PRINT

All the negatives were filed by the assigned production code number. Then all of the stills that were used for promotions in various ways were issued and controlled by the "key set."

When someone wanted a particular still, or it was going to be used for a particular purpose, they pulled the negative to print. Each studio had their own unique marking system, which was primarily based on the intended purpose of the still.

An assignment log was kept to show all the numbers issued in the "Key Set" and how the still was used.

Production Codes Issued

Before we continue, let's take a look at a production code on a still. Some stills would have the studio name and title on the still. That makes it REAL easy. BUT, many of the stills used would not have any identifying information.

Below is an example of a standard still without the studio and title on it and how it was marked. It's from the 1934 MGM film, *Forsaking All Others* starring Clark Gable and Joan Crawford. This was a GREAT still that could be used to create a LOT of buzz.

Now, notice the bottom right corner which is enlarged in the image to the right. You will see a 795-12.

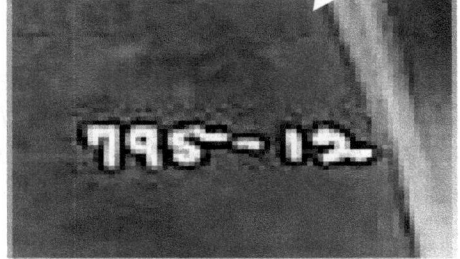

THIS is the production code. The number 795 identifies the MGM production *Forsaking All Others* and the (dash) 12 is the individual still number.

Production codes were not always NUMBERS as shown above. Some studios preferred letters or a letter and number combination. Different studios used slightly different systems.

Some codes are extremely simple to figure out.

For example, most of the Fox Film codes that we have on file from 1917 to 1932 were letter codes. The majority of them were by director.

For example, Frank Borzage directed over 100 films starting back in 1913. In 1925, he went to work for Fox Film and coded all of his films using "BOR" (dash) and a number of that film with Fox. "BOR" was apparently represented the first three letters of his last name.

The image on the following page is a still of Charles Farrell in one of Borzage's most famous films, the 1927 film *7th Heaven*. The marking on the still indicates a production code: BOR-7-38. This code would indicate that this was Borzage's seventh film. The number 38 represents that this was the 38th still processed.

Continuing the pattern, Borzage's sixth film with Fox was the 1926 film *Marriage License* and carried the code Bor-6. His eightth film was *Street Angel* and carried the code Bor-8.

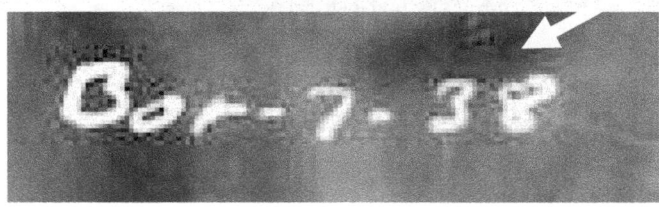

Some codes make perfect sense and some don't. WHY? Because so many changes can happen during filming, editing, post production and final release. Many times in the planning stage, a title would be set based on an important phrase or a book name. In this case, the production code was set with the title codes from the beginning.

But, sometimes the studio was not sure what the final title was going to be. In this case, they would assign a working title and a temporary production code.

On occasion, the production code would be based on a particular star's project, such the "Jack Holt project." For example, the production code number" JH-11" would represent Jack Holt's project #11. Code "JH-11" happens to be the code for the Jack Holt film *Strange Case of Dr. Meade*.

The Publicity Department would then determine if a code conflicted with other projects and how it would be changed. In the case of the above, after editing, a simple addition of the Columbia code was added to become "JH COL-11." The image below shows how the code was changed in this clip of the still for *The Strange Case of Dr. Meade*.

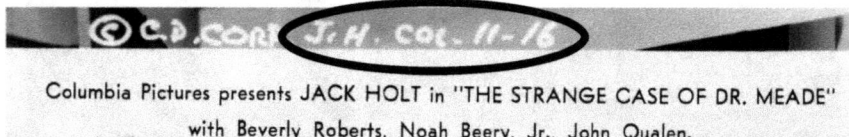

Columbia Pictures presents JACK HOLT in "THE STRANGE CASE OF DR. MEADE" with Beverly Roberts, Noah Beery, Jr., John Qualen.

We call these markings **pre-distribution codes** because they were usually re-numbered in the publicity department once a release title was assigned.

Different Ways the Production Code Was Used

Now let's look at some of the different ways codes were used by the various departments.

Exclusives

Major magazines and publications would quite often want exclusive photos in order to write articles about an upcoming film. This was a tremendous way for the film to get FREE publicity AND give the paper or magazine something exclusive to report on.

To accommodate them, the publicity department would put a hold tag on numerous stills and send over a group for the magazine or newspaper editor to choose from. Once the exclusives were picked, the tags would be removed from those images not selected so they could be used for other purposes.

When researching stills used as "exclusives," we must vary from our "only looking at the front" discussion. For larger and favored publications, the publicity department would choose certain images and enlarge them to 10x13" or 11x14". These larger shots gave the image a more portrait appearance and would quite often win more publicity space.

Here's the good part about "exclusives." They are usually the best of the publicity stills and are normally GREAT shots of the stars.

As for identification, since these are the best shots from the film, it is normally not that difficult to

Notice the sample still below. This "exclusive" still features the adorable Shirley Temple from the 1935 Fox release of *The Little Colonel.* **What a GREAT SHOT!!**

Most of the time, the publicity department did not want the production codes "marring" the photo that was being used in a newspaper or magazine. They would instead write the production code on the BACK of the still, along with any additional information for the paper or magazine. Without the information on the back, if the star happened to be in a couple of "similar"' films, it would become difficult to identify.

Here is the back of the Shirley Temple still:

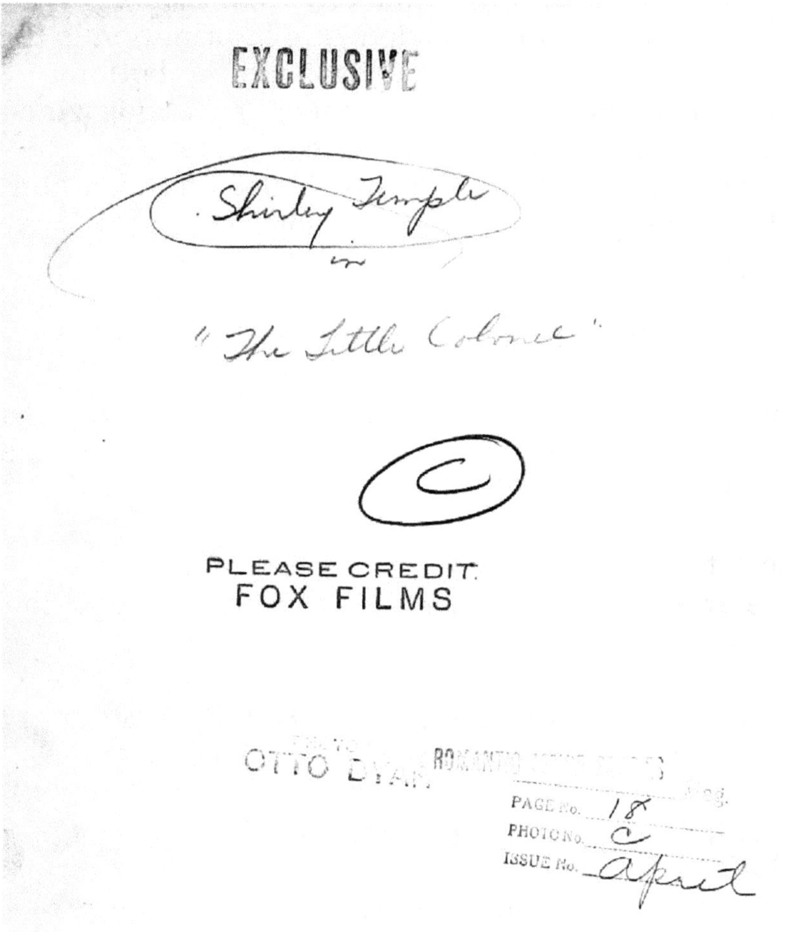

EXCLUSIVE

Shirley Temple
in

"The Little Colonel"

©

PLEASE CREDIT.
FOX FILMS

OTTO DYAR   ROMANTIC

PAGE No. 18
PHOTO No. C
ISSUE No. april

Most studios would stamp "EXCLUSIVE" on the back of the still if it was for a major paper or magazine. That is not the case for smaller publications and it would be used again.

Notice on the back side of the Shirley Temple *The Little Colonel* still seen on the previous page. There is an EXCLUSIVE stamp on the top, This is followed by the name of the star (Shirley Temple) and the film's title (The Little Colonel) in handwriting. There is also a notation to credit Fox Films any time the still is used in a publication. Below this information is the photographer's name (Otto Dyar), On the bottom right side is a stamp with the name of the magazine getting the exclusive rights to use the image (*Romantic Movie Stories*). There is also an indication that the photo will be placed on page 18, photo C in the April issue.

Also notice that in the top left corner is a small number (192-46, which you can't read from the photo). This is the production code with 192 being the number code for *The Little Colonel* and 46 the number for this particular still.

No matter what studio was producing a film, **sometimes** they were in a rush and would forget to mark the stills.

Here is another example from the SAME studio that presents a slightly different problem with exclusives.

The still on the next page features a GREAT shot of Will Rogers playing golf. There are no production codes or markings on the front of the still as was fairly common with most exclusives.

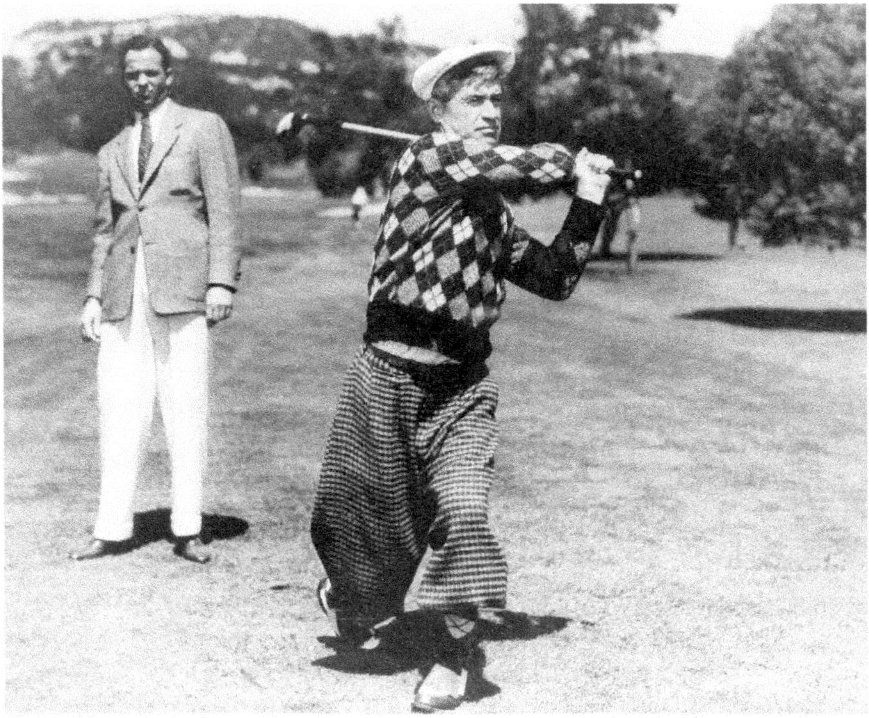

As seen below, the production code was not placed on the back of the still either.

Rogers, Will

EXCLUSIVE

MAY 1934

WILL ROGERS, Fox star,
in a scene from the Fox picture
"Merry Andrew"

PLEASE CREDIT
FOX FILMS

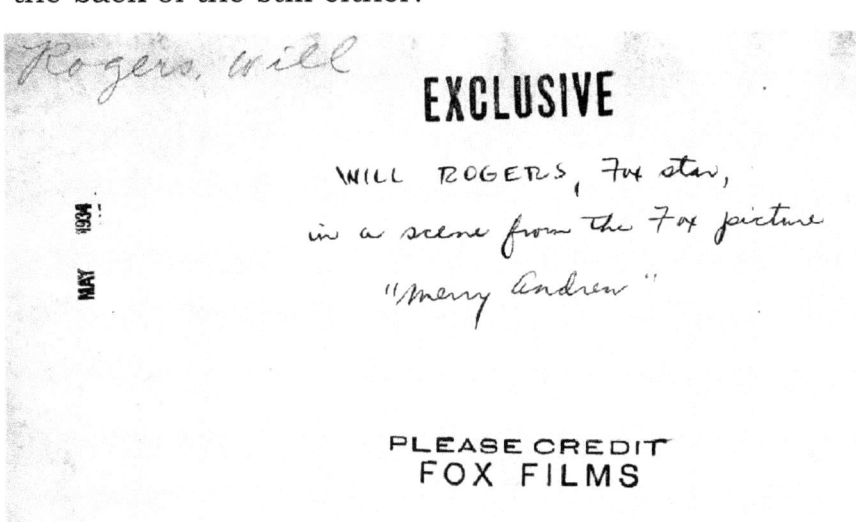

Now let's look at the backside of the Will Rogers' still on the preceding page.

You will see at the top of the backside of the still is the standard "EXCLUSIVE" stamp. This stamp establishes that this photograph was taken and allocated for exclusive use.

Also notice that there is a handwritten note just below the stamp that says: "Will Rogers, Fox star, in a scene from the Fox picture '*Merry Andrew*'". And then there is a date stamp on the left that says "May 1934."

This brings up another common problem with still identification.

These particular stills were taken and sent to the publicity department **during the shooting of the film**. These were used for advance publicity **before the film was released**.

The publicity department tried to create some excitement about the coming release. But it was quite common for a film to have a title change once the film was finished and edited.

In this particular case, the publicity department sent this still out **BEFORE the film was finished** and the final title assigned. ***Merry Andrew*** was actually one of several working titles. The film was actually released as ***Handy Andy***.

The bottom line is that even though a still may have identifying information on the back, there is no guarantee that it is 100% accurate.

Now let's look at a completely DIFFERENT way stills were used to garner publicity.

Portrait Codes

As noted in the discussion of all the jobs of the Unit Photographer (or Special Photographer), some photographs were taken behind the scenes with actors and directors or special set ups for publicity shots. Let's take a closer look at those.

In Chapter 2, we established that executives of the major studios established complete control over all the various steps of the filming process. One of the processes put into place was assigning a CODE for EACH performer.

This number or letter (or combination) was basically an accounting code that would follow an individual through the various stages of employment with the studio. It was used to track what the individual performer did (similar to an employee number and a time clock).

The publicity department also used the same number for several other areas. When they would go through looking for images for the Key Book, they also looked for images that could be used for special promotions. These special promotion shots could also be used BEYOND this particular film's promotions.

The following examples show how stills taken on a specific film with a particular actor or actress were coded and used differently. On the next pages are two stills featuring Merle Oberon from the 1946 film *Temptation*.

Notice the "BD-110" scratched into the bottom left. "BD" is the production code for *Temptation* and 110 is the still number. The film was based on the 1909 novel by Robert Smythe Hichens called *Bella Donna* (BD).

Now, here's another still of Merle Oberon FROM THE SAME FILM.

Notice that on THIS still, the code is "MO-16". "MO" was the portrait code for Merle Oberon.

While production codes were used for scenes in the film, portrait codes were used for accounting purposes AND for photos that could be used for other publicity besides just that particular film.

Most still collectors believe that portrait codes were only for the actors and actresses. That is because the actors and actresses were the main ones seen in the photos. Very few times do you ever see photos of – the cameraman – for example.

Numerous studios used the portrait code for more than just the celebrities. Some also included directors, producers, writers, cameramen and, beyond that (especially at Paramount), **anyone employed by the studio** (craft workers, drama coaches, secretaries, etc.) and anyone connected to a film (the real life subject of a biography, the author of a source novel, etc.).

This ACCOUNTING CODE was used in a WIDE variety of ways. Some codes were even assigned for specific GROUPS of individuals and screen couples that were in the public eye a lot.

Here is a good example of a popular couple where the studio used a separate portrait code.

You should be able to recognize the popular screen couple featured in the still on the next page.   Notice that the bottom right corner of this still has the portrait code of T-H-4, which represents, of course, Spencer Tracy and Katharine Hepburn. Unfortunately, there's no indication of what movie this is from.

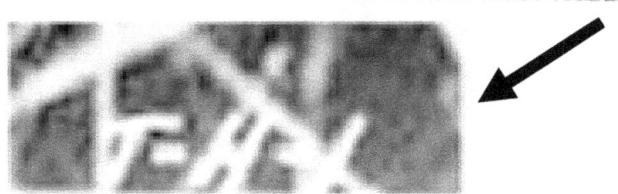

It can be difficult to figure out all of the different uses for portrait codes. Here are some general facts to help.

    A. Portrait codes were primarily used between the 1920s and the 1960s.

    B. When someone left the studio and came back later, a NEW code for that person was usually issued.

    C. Some studios used initials, some used names, some used numbers

    D. Some studios would combine the portrait code with another code such as F or P for fashion or publicity.

    E. Sometimes the code was assigned to a group of stars

    F. Sometimes the studio used initials for their REAL name instead of the stage name.

Since there are so many variables in this area, we will try to address more specific uses later in the book under specific studios.

~~~~~~~~~~

L/R LIMITED RUNS
WWW.LIMITEDRUNS.COM
ORIGINAL VINTAGE POSTERS, PRINT ART & PHOTOGRAPHY

MOVIE ART GmbH

one of Europe's largest selection of movie posters
- silent to present -
over 6000 titles online

Walchestrasse 17
8006 Zurich Switzerland
phone ++41 44 363 50 26
fax ++ 41 44 363 50 27

www.movieart.ch

Jamie at pastposters specializies in Original British Quad Posters Titles from the 1950's until present day.

Also stocking One Sheets, Lobby Cards F.O.H and Press Stills
Plus Press Kits, Press Books and Other Memorabilia

pastposters.com

UK based but ships to over 50 countries worlwide.
Ships Daily To the U.S.A., Australia and Europe

Thousands of Vintage Movie Posters instantly available on a secure website ask to join my weekly mailing list.

support @ pastposters.com
www.pastposters.com

FOUR COLOR COMICS

Posters ~ Comics
Comic Art ~ Books
Magazines ~ Memorabilia

Four Color Comics LLC
Robert Rogovin

P.O. Box 1399
Scarsdale, NY 10583
TEL: (914) 722-4696
FAX: (914) 722-7656

WEB: www.fourcolorcomics.com
EMAIL: rob@fourcolorcomics.com

DOMINIQUE BESSON AFFICHES

220 Chemin de la Blanchère - 84270 Vedène - France

TEL : 33.613.451.355   -   FAX : 33.442.634.188

WEB : www.dominiquebesson.com

E-MAIL : info@dominiquebesson.com

CATALOGUE

ON

REQUEST

CHAPTER 5

ADVERTISING DEPARTMENT

The advertising department was responsible for developing and initiating the advertising budget to be used for promoting the film. Once the budget was established, the advertising department would outline their complete advertising campaign.

The black & white and color stills provided by the publicity department would be used in a number of ways, including the following.

Creation of Posters

The advertising department would select certain stills and provide them, along with a synopsis of the film, to the art department. It was the art department's responsibility to design and complete the poster art and other advertising material, either using in-house staff or contracting with a commercial artist.

Creation of Lobby Cards

The art department would also pick through the color stills provided by the publicity department to create the lobby cards and other color promotional material. Normally, the production code was removed to create the U.S. lobby cards, but occasionally, someone would slip up and leave the number on.

The following shows a lobby card for the 1961 sci-fi release *Gorgo*. The production code number ("GO-42") can be see on the bottom right.

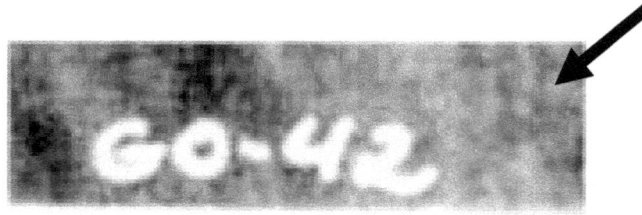

It was more common to see production codes on international material. It was up to the distributor in whatever country was releasing the film whether the production code remained on their lobby cards.

Here is an example.

The following image features a still from the 1933 film *Duck Soup* starring the Marx Brothers. The production code 1453 can be seen in the bottom right.

On the Australian lobby card pictured below, the 1453 production code can be seen on the bottom right corner of the card.

Creation of Advertising Clips

The advertising department would use both stills and artwork provided by the art department to create the ad mats that were used in magazines and by the theater managers to promote the film locally.

In the silent and early "talkie" years, this artwork would be sent to contracted companies to produce the ads on wood blocks that could be ordered by the theater and sent to the local newspapers for publication. This was replaced by the lighter plates and then eventually by ad supplements that had clip art that the theater could send to the newspaper.

Press

Prior to distribution rights being given to the National Screen Service ("NSS"), the advertising department would offer sets of stills to individual theaters for their use in advertising a specific film. When NSS took over the distribution of movie paper for the major studios, it would offer press stills to theaters and exhibitors along with the other sizes and types of movie posters and promotional materials. Beginning in the 1970's, press stills became a part of the press kits that were distributed by NSS.

New York Newspaper Set

Starting in the 1960's, the advertising department provided a basic pack of stills, referred to as "The New York Newspaper Set," to wire services and newspapers around the country. This set included 30-40 stills selected from the key set.

~~~~~~~~~~

Movie Poster Frames
Direct from Studio Supplier

Specializing in framing your collectibles since 1984

Made to order custom frames
At Wholesale Prices
~ Delivered to your door ~

www.hollywoodposterframes.com
(800) 463-2994

9260 Deering Ave
Chatsworth, CA 91311

Open to public:
Thur-Fri: 10-5 p.m.
Sat: 9-2 p.m.

channingposters

**ORIGINAL
MOVIE POSTERS,
LOBBY CARDS, AND
AUTOGRAPHED ITEMS**

**CHANNING THOMSON
P. O. BOX 330232
SAN FRANCISCO, CA 94133-0232**

Email: channinglylethomson@att.net
ebay: http://stores.ebay.com/CHANNINGPOSTERS

Also the home of PosterParty.com!

Movie Posters ~ Music Posters
TV Posters ~ Celebrity Posters
Star Wars & James Bond
Harry Potter

Collectormania
17892 Cottonwood Dr
Parker, CO 80134

1-866-630-1648

questions@posterplanet.net
posterplanetfile@aol.com

Bonhams

Entertainment Memorabilia

Consignments now invited for upcoming auctions

Norma Shearer's *Marie Antoinette* albums
Sold for $34,160

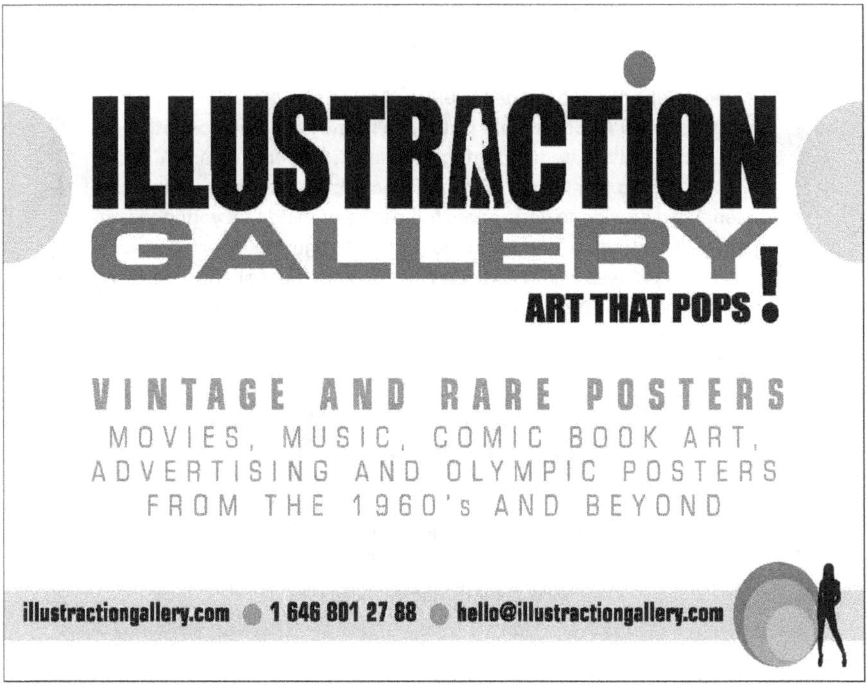

+1 (323) 436 5467
International auctioneers and appraisers · bonhams.com/entertainment

---

ILLUSTRACTION GALLERY!
ART THAT POPS!

VINTAGE AND RARE POSTERS
MOVIES, MUSIC, COMIC BOOK ART,
ADVERTISING AND OLYMPIC POSTERS
FROM THE 1960's AND BEYOND

illustractiongallery.com • 1 646 801 27 88 • hello@illustractiongallery.com

WANTED: CONSIGNMENTS!

Robert Edward Auctions is currently seeking consignments for inclusion in our next auction. If you have a significant high value item or collection that you are considering selling at auction, you can't afford **NOT** to contact **Robert Edward Auctions**. For more than 30 years Robert Edward Auctions has offered an unparalleled tradition of integrity, knowledge and professionalism. **Robert Edward Auctions** offers the ultimate auction service and is exclusively geared to high quality material. Larger circulation + unparalleled knowledge and experience + lower commission rates = more money in your pocket. Robert Edward Auctions also offers: Reasonable reserves, unmatched financial security (millions in assets, NO liabilities), millions of dollars available at all times at a moment's notice for cash advances, and the most extensive list of buyers in the collecting world. **Robert Edward Auctions will put more money in your pocket.** If you have high quality material to bring to auction, Robert Edward Auctions will not only help you realize the highest possible prices for your valuable material, we provide to consignors the peace of mind that your consignments will be treated with the utmost in care, and that every aspect of the auction process will be executed with the greatest attention to every detail. If you have high quality material you think might be of interest, please call or write.

ROBERT EDWARD AUCTIONS, LLC.
P.O. Box 7256 • Watchung, NJ 07069
phone: 908-226-9900 fax: 908-226-9920
www.RobertEdwardAuctions.com

CHAPTER 6
SPECIAL PHOTOGRAPHER

Under certain circumstances, particularly with some major films, specially contracted photographers were used. For example, some actors and actresses would prefer their own photographers to take special promotional shots. These photographers were allowed on the set for major scenes or at the end of the day's shooting where the star would recreate a certain scene or pose for publicity purposes.

Sometimes a specific publication that was going to do a major feature on an upcoming film would send down its own special photographer. In these instances, it was a common practice that the photographer would own the rights to the shots they took. Instead of any payment from the studio, the special photographers would mark their stills and charge royalties for any outside use.

This practice caused some major lawsuits and confusion over the years. Some of the photographers OWNED the photographs they took during the filming of a major film title. These photographers later allowed their photographs to go into public domain, while the studio renewed the copyrights on all the photographs that the unit photographer took.

Special photographers would normally have their stamp on the photo.

Below are two samples of individual photographer tags that were placed on their prints.

Most of the time, very little information was placed on the back of the photographer prints. If there was, the type and amount of information would vary.

From time to time, a studio would request the use of one or more of the special photographer's images. These images would be marked and incorporated into the key set or other press materials, with the permission of the special photographer and with the photographer's name on the back.

Let's take a look at the still on the next page which is from the 1927 Fox film *Sunrise*. This photograph was taken by the unit photographer.

This Key Set still (indicated by the two holes on the left) features the title and basic credit information. It has the production code of "M-1" with a dash and still number 66.

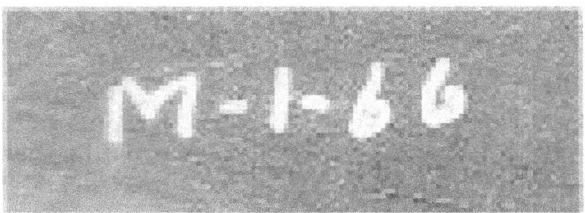

Now let's look at another still from the same film on the next page. This photograph was taken by a special photographer and used by the studio.

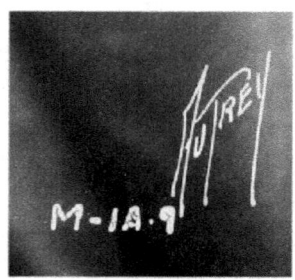

WILLIAM FOX presents SUNRISE F.W. MURNAU'S production

The still on the preceding page has all the same title and credit information of the still on page 67, but this one has the Special Photographer's (Max Munn Autrey) signature.

The production number has also been changed from "M-1" to "M-1A." The addition of the "A" represents the photographer Autrey.

Let's look at a different way that the photographs taken by the Special Photographer were used by the studios to garner some extra publicity about an upcoming film.

The still on the next page was utilized by the FASHION department. It features Gloria Swanson in the 1934 film *Music in the Air*. (It has the two hole punches at the top which means it was part of the Key Book Set).

Notice that the still number in the bottom right is "10." This was a special publicity photo shot after production shooting for the day was finished which was used for a special promotion. Consequently, there is no production code number.

The fashion department used this photograph to promote Miss Swanson's gown, which was designed by Rene Hubert, The image was published in a fashion magazine article about the upcoming film.

It has a write up on the back with a stamp giving the image credit to photographer Otto Dyar. See image of back on page 71.

GLORIA SWANSON

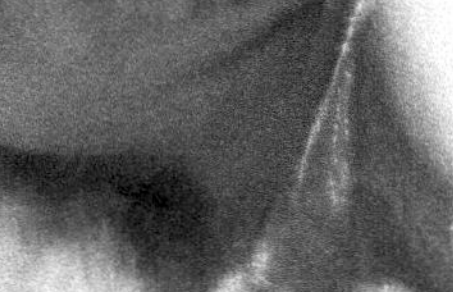

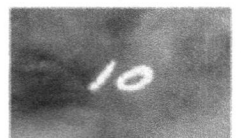

Gracious in line is this Rene Hubert inspired creation worn by Gloria Swanson in "Music In The Air," Fox Film production, in which she co-stars with John Boles. On an ivory silk crepe foundation tiny ivory satin bugle beads were sewn by hand until they covered every inch of the fabric. A molded silhouette, with a normal waistline, marked by a simple belt of the beaded crepe, the decolletage is high in front and is V-shaped in the back to the waist. The long sleeves, form-fitting on the forearm expand to cape-like fullness on the upper arm. A long train adds charm to the skirt. A novelty decorative effect is introduced by means of the emerald green crystal beads in semi-necklace effect with diamond clasps. A bracelet on the left wrist repeats the jewel-theme. Slippers are white silk crepe.

The close-fitting cap, also designed and created by Rene Hubert, Fox Film stylist, repeats the dress materials and is further enhanced by the use of two elaborate clasps at either side.

And finally, let's look at a very popular way that they studio could use the Special Photographer to not only get some publicity about the film – BUT to also get some additional money at the same time – Promotional Tie-ins.

A promotional tie-in would take a special shot of a star or scene and tie it in with a commercial product.

In the above still from the 1936 Warner Bros. film, *Two Against the World*, starring Humphrey Bogart, Bogie is promoting Lektrolite cigarette lighters.

~~~~~~~~~~~

FILM/ART
Original Film Posters

Hollywood, CA

323.363.2969

filmartgallery.com

SPOTLIGHTDISPLAYS.COM

**ORIGINAL MOVIE POSTERS,
LOBBY CARDS,
MOVIE STILLS
AND MEMORABILIA**

JOHN REID VINTAGE MOVIE MEMORABILIA
PO Box 92 -- Elanora -- Qld 4221 -- Australia

info@moviemem.com
http://www.moviemem.com
ebay userid: johnwr

Original Poster
.co.uk

Original Vintage Film Posters - For Sale.

British quads, US & UK one sheets, animation art, front of house and lobby cards.

Over 7,000 posters and lobby cards available online!

info@originalposter.co.uk
UK Callers 01905 620 370
Int Callers +44 1905 620370

High quality shipping tubes for Vintage Posters.

*95 sizes in stock. Immediate Shipment.
End Plugs Included. One box minimum.
Credit Cards Accepted.*

YAZOO MILLS, INC.
MANUFACTURERS OF PAPER TUBES AND CORES
P.O. BOX 369 • NEW OXFORD, PA 17350

CALL TOLL FREE 1-800-242-5216 FAX 717-624-4420

ORDER ONLINE
www.yazoomills.com

CHAPTER 7

OUTSIDE THE MAJOR STUDIO FRAMEWORK

The "production code" was originally created to help track production through the filming process. However, as seen in earlier chapters, the major studios expanded it into an accounting code, a publicity code, a distribution code, a portrait code, and even an employee number.

The production code became utilized in a lot of the departments. The major studios had all of the departments to handle every step of the process, so inter-department codes are no problem.

Once you move outside of the major studio system though, things do not work quite the same. So let's take a look at some of them.

The Independents

Independent production companies usually didn't have advertising departments, art departments, publicity departments, etc. They rarely dealt with anything like special photographers and exclusives.

During the planning stage, the production code would be established. It might be the director's initials, the stars' initials, a character series, or whatever code that was decided on for that film. Whatever it was, it was normally put on the stills very similar to the system described earlier except on a smaller basis.

If the production company already had a distributor, they would send over the stills and the distributor would handle the other areas. If the production company DIDN'T have a distributor, then the best stills were picked out and used to create a package to present a potential distributor.

If no distributor was signed before the end of the production, then material was compiled and decisions made on how to promote the film. In this case, distribution was normally handled through states rights or roadshow. For later releases, distribution would also include film festivals.

The two largest independent production companies were Hal Roach and Mack Sennett, with each producing films for multiple distributors. Both were monsters in the industry and had completely different ways of marking their productions. Here's how they each handled their production codes

Hal Roach

Hal Roach started producing films in 1914. He didn't have a distributor, so he formed his own company called Rolin. In 1915, he did several tests for major distributors such as Pathe and Universal. For these, he marked the stills with a letter and number.

Pathe liked his material, and in 1915 started distributing a new series called Lonesome Luke under the banner of Phun Philms. For this series, Roach started marking them all with a prefix of "P" (P-1, P-2, P-3, etc.). After the first 30, he restarted the numbering with a prefix of "A."

With every new series that he started, he would begin marking the stills with a different letter and a number. So, ALL Hal Roach stills usually carry a single letter (dash) number and then the still number OR an additional HR and THEN the letter and number.

If you are just picking up Hal Roach stills occasionally, this can be EXTREMELY confusing. **Why, you say?** Let me give you an example.

In 1917, Roach started a series for Pathe beginning with A-1. In 1922, he started a new Our Gang series directed by McCowan with A-1. In 1931, he started a new ZaSu Pitts and Thelma Todd series for MGM with A-1. So you have three different series starting with A-1. This pattern continued into the mid A-30s.

This was done with almost **every letter**. When Roach wanted to start a new series, he would pick a letter he hadn't used in a while and use it again.

The only letters that he didn't use were I, N, O, Q, U, V, W, X, Y and Z. All others were on multiple series starting with the number "1," except for the letter "J". In 1923, Roach started a series of Rex the Wonder Horse feature films for Pathe that was directed by Fred Jackman. From 1923 – 1927, five feature films were produced under the "J" series.

In the early 1930's, before dubbing, Roach would put an additional letter behind the production code to show what language, such as: "E-English"; "S-Spanish": "F-French"; etc.

We have a comprehensive breakdown of all of the confusing Hal Roach series in our *Movie Still Identification Book* and online in our member section of www.MovieStillID.com.

Mack Sennett

Mack Sennett was financed by New York Motion Picture Co. in 1912 to form Keystone Studios. In 1915, Sennett, D. W. Griffith and Thomas Ince formed Triangle Films.

At the collapse of Triangle in 1917, Sennett formed Mack Sennett Comedies and distributed through Paramount, Pathe, Educational, and several others. During his life, Sennett acted in 360 films, directed over 300 films and produced over 1100 films.

Once Sennett started using production codes, he used all numbers unless it was marked for specific distributors. But with that being said, it can get very confusing because of two major factors:

1. Sennett films came in during the development of production codes so many of his early films did not utilize them.

2. Because Sennett supplied different distributors, most of them added their own codes as well, creating multiple codes on many of the titles.

Mack Sennett produced Keystone productions for Mutual starting in 1915. These films used a code starting with a "K" and then a number. Mack Sennett formed Mack Sennett Comedies in 1917 that used numbers with no letter prefix.

Triangle started using codes in 1915 with the letter "T" followed by a number. Triangle Komedies were given AN ADDITIONAL code that started with an "X." Sometimes BOTH "T" and "X" were used.

When Keystone started providing films to Triangle, there would be a Keystone code "K," a Triangle code "T" and/or an additional Triangle Komedy code "X."

There is an additional oddity on some Mack Sennett stills. Occasionally, there appears to be an additional set of numbers included in the production code.

In 1932-33, Sennett produced 19 comedy shorts for Paramount Publix. We have located a still for the 1933 film *The Singing Boxer*. The still does NOT have any Paramount Publix or ANY markings on it. But, instead of the standard Mack Sennett production code, it has the code of "MS-18."

Only 3 of the 19 shorts were produced in 1933 and this looks like the 18th of the 19 films (which would make sense). But is this a reissue after Paramount Publix was absorbed that was marked with an "MS?" We have not verified either way yet.

A review of these two major independents shows that they marked their productions differently but used the same basic principles.

Now, let's take a look at distribution companies and how production codes were used.

Distribution Companies

Outside the major studios, the term should actually be changed to production and distribution code, because the DISTRIBUTOR had total control over the code number. It is the distributor's name that the film was listed under and NOT the production company.

It was at the discretion of the distributor to: (1) keep the number assigned by the film's producer; (2) assign another number; or (3) eliminate the number entirely. This situation creates additional complications.

The distributor was normally promoting material from a wide variety of sources. It could be a steady client, a one-time customer, an import film or even rights to distribute a re-release.

Because of this, quite often it appears the distributor would re-number the stills to fit into THEIR accounting system. So it is not unusual to see either two or more sets of codes OR no codes at all.

So let's look at a film released in 1949 by Verity Films, a small U.S. distributor. [NOTE: In our example, we are NOT trying to identify the still but simply showing the process.]

Verity had acquired the rights to rerelease a Paramount film called *Beachcomber* starring Charles Laughton. Paramount had originally released the film in 1938, but had acquired it from Associated British Film Distributors, a British film distributor.

The film was originally released in the U,K, under the title *Vessel of Wrath*. Paramount got it the same year and changed the title. Ten years later, a small distributor, Verity, wanted to rerelease the film.

Sounds simple enough – right?

The image on the next page features six press stills from the 1949 re-release of the film *The Beachcomber* by Verity Films, Inc. Verity used National Screen Service ("NSS") for paper and accessory distribution. As such, the still contains the standard NSS studio tag across the bottom of each as well as the title and film information. There is also an NSS number (49/94) in the bottom right of each border tag.

Now ALL of these stills were issued through NSS in 1949, but one of these stills differs from the rest.

All the stills have the production code number 1776 and then the still number. BUT, one still has some additional information. This particular still has two additional code numbers: the 1776 on the right and the VW 131 just above it.

Since the original title was *Vessel of Wrath* ("VW"), this was apparently put on the still by the original DISTRIBUTOR, which was Associated British Film Distributors (ABFD).

Also notice that on the left of the still is the marking "MF.1/540." The production company was Mayflower Pictures. This happens to be the first film that we have on record for them. The assumption is that the MF-1 would be for MayFlower 1, making this the original production code.

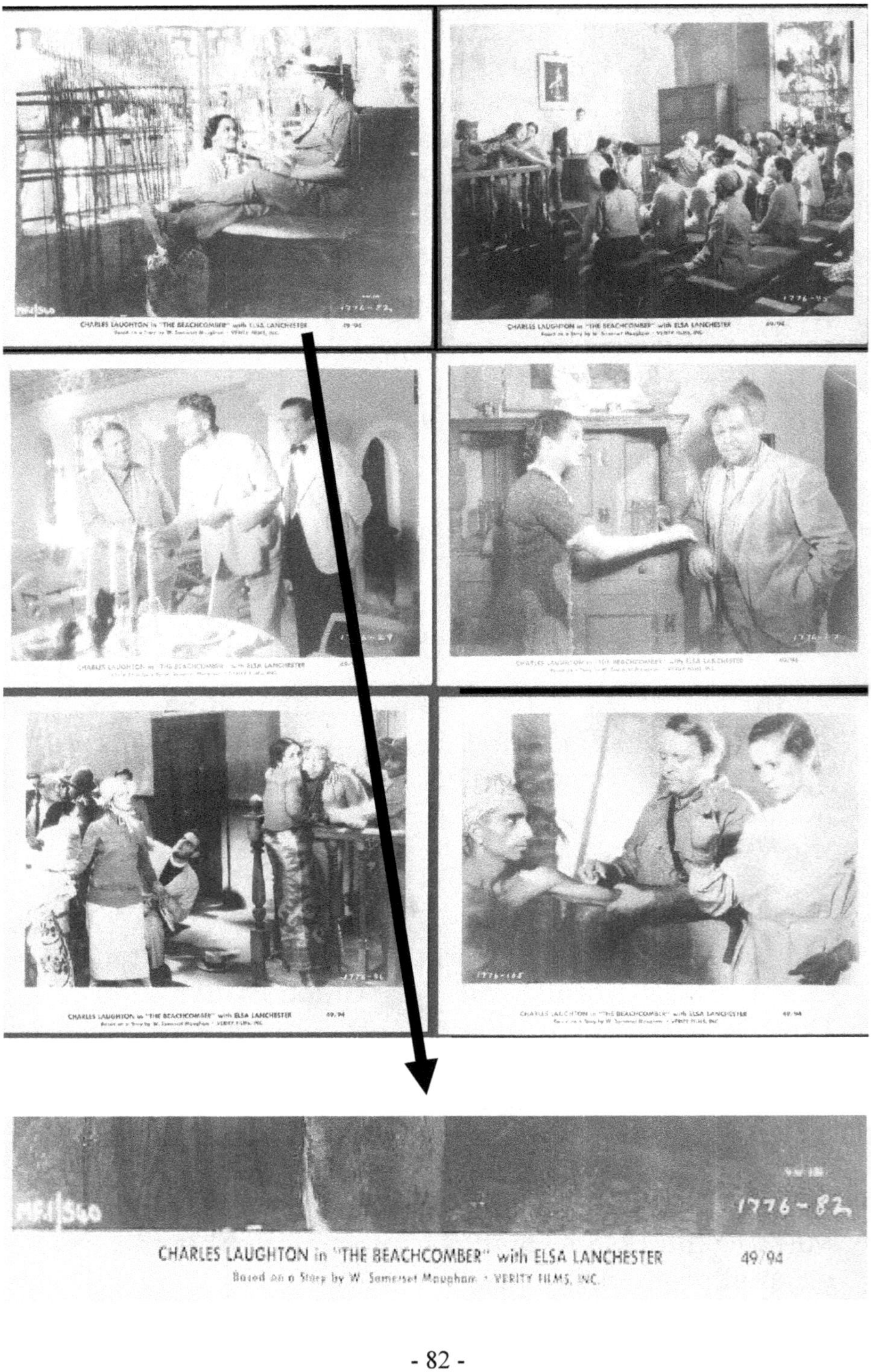
MFI/560
1776-82
CHARLES LAUGHTON in "THE BEACHCOMBER" with ELSA LANCHESTER 49/94
Based on a Story by W. Somerset Maugham • VERITY FILMS, INC.

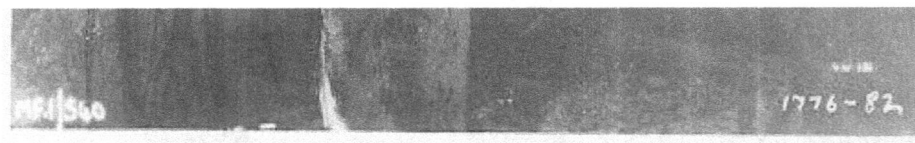

The point of this example is to show that every time the stills were handled by a different distributor, the production codes were added and/or taken away at the discretion of that distributor.

Now we can't do a section on film distributors without at least mentioning the largest distributor of film stills and accessories at that time - the National Screen Service.

National Screen Service

And I can already hear the questions – the National Screen Service ("NSS") identified all of their stills so WHY would we need to look at them? This will be addressed in detail in the next chapter.

The National Screen Service started in 1920. They developed their number system in 1930 for trailers and then modified it to include all other film accessories (posters, stills, pressbooks, etc.) in 1940.

NSS dominated the distribution of stills for all the major studios all the way into the 1980s. Collectors, researchers and archivists owe NSS a HUGE amount of kudos for categorizing, marking and keeping control of such a massive amount of material in a way that could be easily researched with their accounting system.

Their numbering system is on a lot of stills, like the set above, so you need be able to recognize what is and what isn't an NSS number.

Also, you can't get TOO comfortable with NSS stills. But, instead of addressing it here, in the next chapter, we will be addressing some common problems to all studios, and notice how many of them are on NSS stills.

If you are not familiar with NSS, we have several books available on National Screen Service at www.LearnAboutMoviePosters.com ("LAMP").

There is also a massive amount of NSS information in our members area of LAMP.

~~~~~~~~~~

THE CINEMATRADE.COM

Your source for original posters and memorabilia

Classics to current... and everything in between

BUY - SELL - TRADE

SEARCH & SPECIAL ORDER

thewildbunch@yahoo.com

Conway's Vintage Treasures

Vintage Movie Posters * Rare Vintage Stills
Rare Autographs * Classic Sports Artifacts
Historical Memorabilia * Fine Art

www.CVTreasures.com
Kevin@CVTreasures.com
866-499-8112

Femmes Fatales & Fantasies

Visit our Museum/Gallery
Femmes Fatales & Fantasies
7013 E. Main Street
Scottsdale, AZ 85251
480.429.6800

Intemporel Gallery opened in 1982. We specialize in vintage movie posters.

22 rue Saint-Martin
Paris, 75004 France
Phone: 1.42.72.55.41

email: choko@intemporel.com
website: www.intemporel.com

THE LAST MOVING PICTURE COMPANY

Morris Everett, Jr
10535 Chillicothe Rd.
Kirtland, OH 44094
Phone: 440-256-3660
Email: lastmo@aol.com
Web: www.hollywoodposterauction.com

L'Imagerie gallery

- ♥ ORIGINAL VINTAGE MOVIE POSTERS
- ♥ RARE FILM POSTERS BOUGHT AND SOLD
- ♥ LINENBACKING AND RESTORATION SERVICES
- ♥ EXPERT CUSTOM FRAMING

L'IMAGERIE ART GALLERY
In Business Since 1973

www.limageriegallery.com

PHONE: 818-762-8488   FAX: 818-762-8499   EMAIL: limageriegallery@gmail.com

10555 Victory Boulevard - North Hollywood, CA 91606
Tuesday through Saturday from 11:30 to 6:00

Fun! Fun! Fun!

Near Mint & Mint

Vintage 1940's - 80's

US Movie Posters

Wholesale to the Public

www.amazing3rdplanet.com

Money Back Guarantee
Dealer enquiries welcome

CHAPTER 8

COMMON PROBLEMS WITH ALL STUDIOS

When we created our first production code book in 2007, it had 18,000 codes and was developed completely from lists that we had acquired from several reputable sources. Since that time, we have been continually modifying and expanding the original lists because we were USING THEM as we were going through literally tens of thousands of stills.

Our *2013 Movie Still Identification Book* has 45,400 production codes and the VAST majority were taken directly from the stills. And I can tell you that taking them DIRECTLY from the images has shown every kind of crazy variation imaginable. Because of this, we think it would be beneficial for YOU to see a couple of the oddities that were common to all studios and might help you understand some of the unusual marks that you might see.

When you first start using production code numbers, you will immediately recognize the huge amount of inconsistencies. We gathered these codes from a WIDE variety of sources, such as studio records, lists from dealers and collectors AND going through tens of thousands of stills. BUT, the problem isn't from the wide variety of sources: the problem is within the studio system.

These codes were used for control at THAT particular time for THAT particular purpose. They didn't take into consideration that maybe different people who created different stills from the Key Set would write the numbers differently, OR that when the distributor remade the stills for press releases, they would write it a different way, OR, if it was redistributed later by a different distributor, or even a distributor in a different country, that the codes would become slightly different.

You have to remember that at the time these stills were originally released, people were just doing their job and there was NEVER EVER a single thought that MAYBE... 40... 50... 60 ... or more years down the road someone might have trouble figuring out what this still was. Their only thought was to do their job and promote the film.

We've learned some very important lessons while compiling production codes. When oddities arise, you basically have to be a detective to search for clues. Sometimes it is written one way and then another. If you don't find it under one listing, try it under a slight variation, etc.

When we first started, I thought that I would just contact the studio archives and they could quickly clear up any problems. So, my first encounter was trying to identify some cast members on some early stills from the teens.

The stills had a studio stamp, the title, a recognizable star, a well-known director and a good production code number, so we "thought" this wouldn't be too much of a problem.

After our initial search, none of the regular sources had the cast members, so we contacted the studio archivist. We sent over the title and production code and received a shocking report:

THEY HAD NO RECORD OF THAT PRODUCTION EVER BEING MADE THERE.

We said: "Wait, here's a copy of the stills with the studio stamp and you can see the production codes!" The studio archivist said:

WE HAVE NO RECORD OF THAT.

After some additional discussions, we came to the conclusion that it was fairly common for the production company to use their own system and THEN the studio would completely re-number and re-title the project.

The problem is that the documentation during production was basically eliminated and NO records kept. Sometimes, identifying pre-release stills CAN GIVE YOU NIGHTMARES!

Here are some other examples common to all studios:

Problems With NSS Number Confusion

Since we were just talking about National Screen Service, let's start off with an NSS problem.

The images on the following pages feature stills from the classic musical *The Sound of Music*, starring Julie Andrews and Christopher Plummer.

20th Century-Fox Presents
"THE SOUND OF MUSIC"
A Robert Wise Production
Filmed in Todd-AO and DeLuxe Color

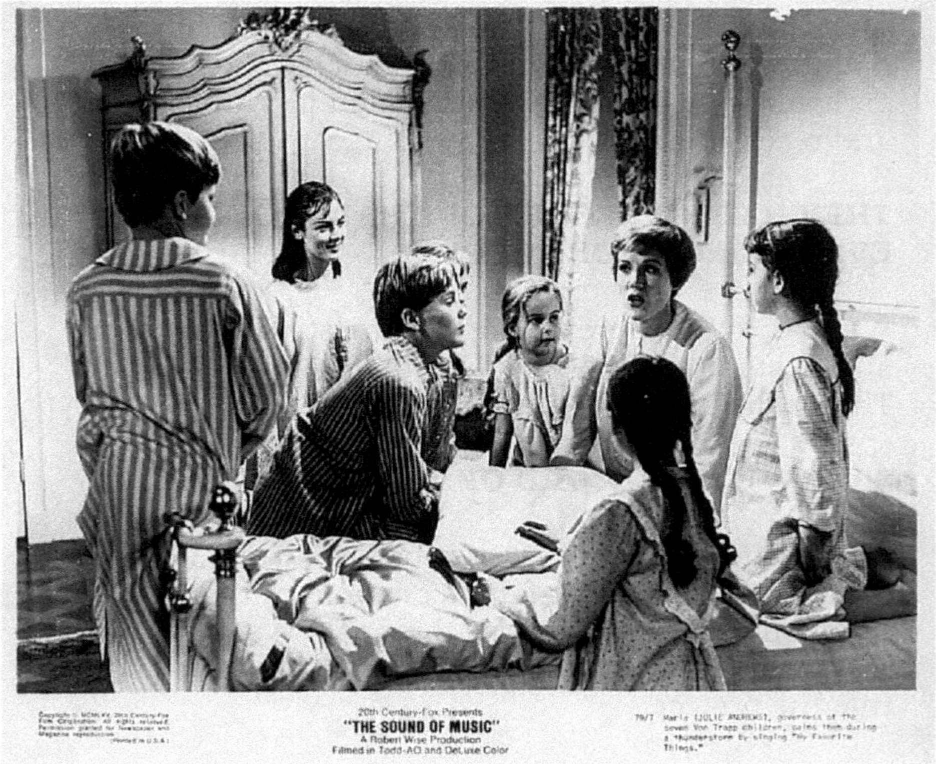

Below is a close up of the bottom of the still.

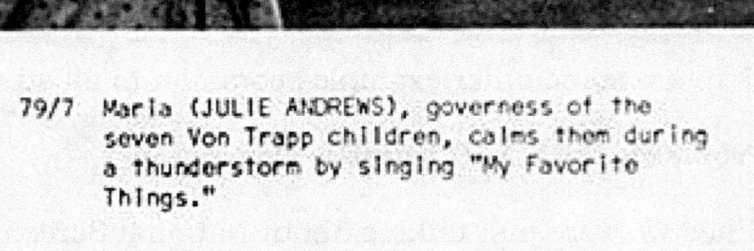

79/7 Maria (JULIE ANDREWS), governess of the seven Von Trapp children, calms them during a thunderstorm by singing "My Favorite Things."

If you asked poster collectors, the majority would say that the 79/7 is the NSS number.

That is until you showed them another still from the film, such as the one on the next page.

Below is a close up of the bottom of the still.

79/44 Julie Andrews, Christopher Plummer and the seven children sing at the Salzburg Music Festival prior to their escape from the Nazis.

It shows the number 79/44. That's right. 79 is the production code number and NOT the NSS number.

In the 1960s, some studios started "printing" production codes with still descriptions on **some** of the stills. It wasn't consistent. This practice gained popularity and is now the norm for a lot of newer stills distributors, such as Disney.

Mistakes on Studio Issued Stills

Here is a problem that happens often and is rarely caught except for major films. When studios send out their press materials, it would be expected that their employees would know what they are doing, or at least know when something is blatantly wrong. Collectors rely on the studio tag and rarely double check the production code number to make sure.

Check out the following still from the award winning film *Guess Who's Coming To Dinner* starring Spencer Tracy and Sidney Poitier:

Sidney Poitier doesn't quite look like himself in this shot. According to the production code, this still is for the film *Captain's Courageous*.

Here's another still from *Guess Who's Coming To Dinner*.

Sidney Poitier looked at lot like Mickey Rooney when he was a child. Anyway, you get the point.

When mistakes like this occur on a major title that everyone knows, it is easy to spot the wrong still. But this is not the case when it involves a lesser known title. These stills are normally just passed through because we have a tendency to think that the studio would know their own material.

The point is this. Just because it is issued by the studio doesn't automatically make it correct. The production code on this still clearly states that it is *Boy's Town*. So, it's good to always check the production code as well.

Multiple Production Code Numbers on Stills

We touched early on a problem of multiple numbers under Independent Distributors. Let's revisit this point, as it was not just an independent distributor problem, but a problem for ALL distributors that handled imports. While we are at it, with our next sample, we can also cover copyright tags.

Shown on the next page are some stills for the 1972 re-release of Charlie Chaplin's *Limelight*.

These stills were distributed by National Screen Service and all of the stills have the NSS service tag and number (72/26) on the bottom right.

All of them also have the production code "L" for *Limelight*.

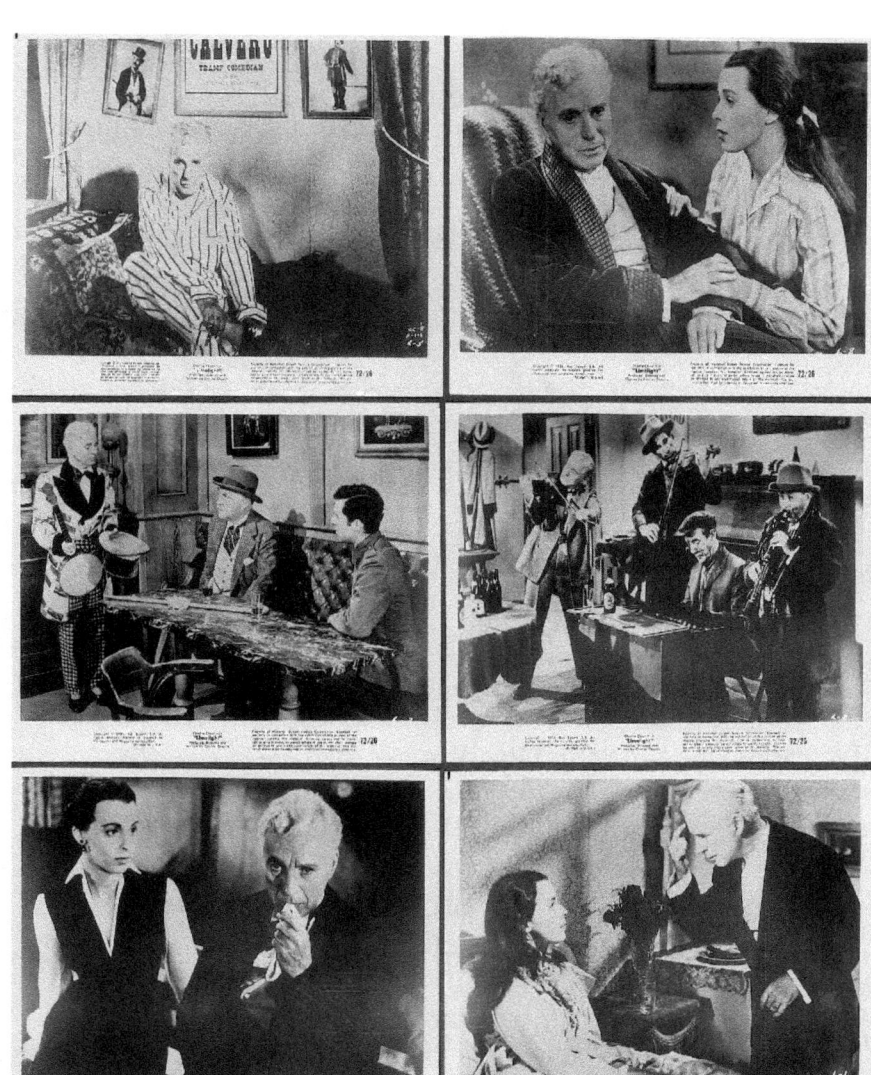

What you can't see is that three of the six have a 1956 copyright on the left with no studio (which is odd since the original release came out in 1952). The other three stills have a 1972 copyright by Columbia Pictures.

REMEMBER: ALL 6 have the 1972 NSS tag and number.

Now let's look closer at the top left still, which you can plainly see has 3 production codes in the right corner.

L-5 is the production code for *Limelight*; CC-8 is bound to be Charlie Chaplin -8, but P-116 – No clue.

We already learned in the Independent Distributor section that every time the stills were handled by a different distributor, the production codes were added and/or taken away at the discretion of that distributor. But now we can add that the copyright tags went along with it also.

Original vs. Reissued Stills

One of the biggest problems with production codes is identifying reissues from originals. When a studio reissues their own film, they just pull the material and send it out again. So, it is almost impossible to tell which release it is from. You can hope that they put different copyright tags on them, but as you saw in the last example, that's not that accurate either.

Only one major studio went out of their way to renumber their reissues. We cover that in the next chapter on individual studios. The best hope that we currently have is that the reissue was by a different distributor leaving their own mark.

I understand that there is a company in New York trying to come up with a way of dating newer stills by the chemicals that were used to develop them, but I haven't heard any real results yet.

Handwriting Mistakes

Here are a couple of clips from the film, *Hannie Caulder*.

The production code for *Hannie Caulder* is "HC." "HC" = **H**annie **C**aulder - that seems fairly simple. We have gone through a lot of *Hannie Caulder* stills and they were all the same with one exception.

The image below features an enlarged view of the bottom of a still from *Hannie Caulder*. It clearly shows the "HC" code.

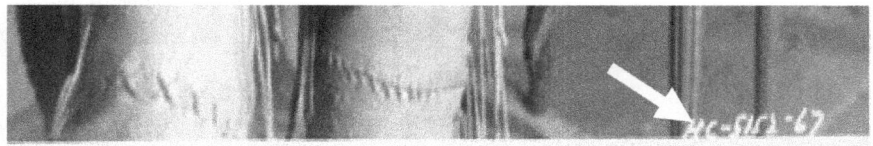

Now let's look at the still clip on the next page.

The following image also shows an enlarged view of the bottom of a still from *Hannie Caulder*. But this one, for some reason, shows the code as "MC"???

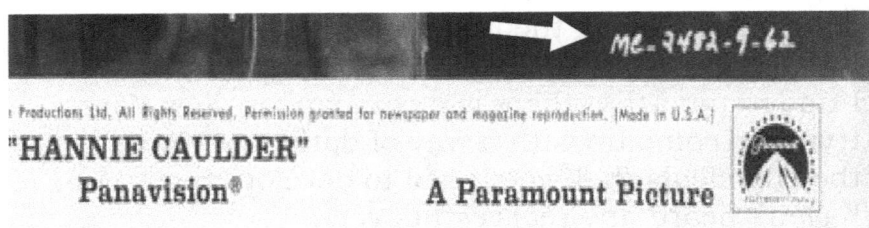

This mistake was probably due to a studio employee copying the code from another still, mistaking the "H" for a "M.". The problem is that if you only had the one still, you would not notice the error.

Backwards Printing

Here's a clip of a still from the film *The Bride Wore Red*.

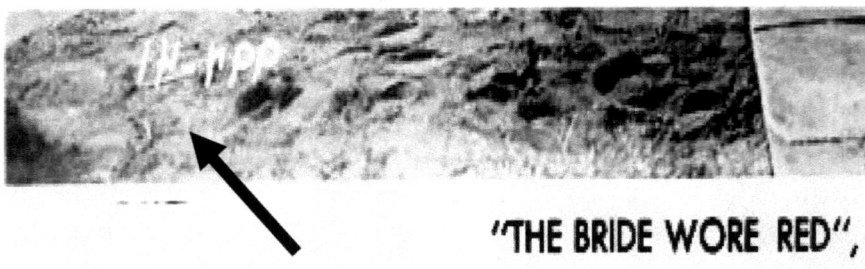

The production code number is actually "997," which you would see if you hold the still up to a mirror. The code is BACKWARDS.

Numbers Chopped

The next clip is taken from a still for the film The Incredible Shrinking Man. Fortunately, this is a popular film and should be recognizable to most. However, there is NO identification on the front of the still, and all you have is the production code (which you can see is 828)

Unfortunately, if the identification of THIS particular still was based solely on the production code, it would remain unidentified. Here's why.

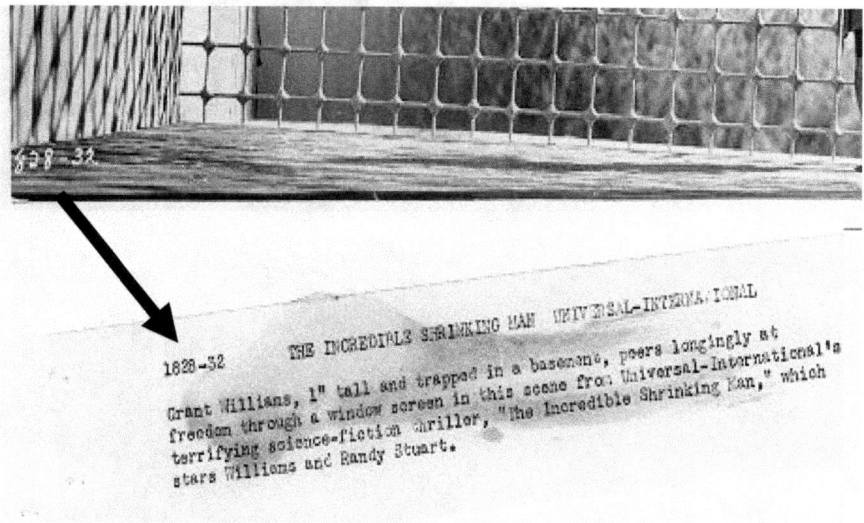

The production code on the still, "828" was actually **chopped** at printing. The actual production code, as seen on the snipe that was attached to the back of the still, is "1828." Fortunately, in this particular instance, there was a studio clip on the back side.

Always beware when the production code is very close to the edge, as there is no telling how much could be **CHOPPED!**

That Little Black Box

We have been asked many times about the little black boxes found on some stills. Here is a sample of a still from the Marilyn Monroe film, *Don't Bother to Knock*. Notice the black box at the bottom right of the still, which has the production code in it.

Now here is another still from the same film, BUT NOTICE, the black box is on the top right.

So WHY the black box, and does the placement mean anything. i.e. produced in different locations or edited for different reasons, etc? Let's first address the black box.

In Chapter 4, we discussed the marking of stills by the Publicity Department in the making of the Key Set. Occasionally, the production codes would have to be revised AFTER they were etched on a still. The best way to make these changes was to create a black background and make a new one. Yes, these were initially created to make changes.

Some studios picked up the process to become a regular spot instead of scratching them into the still.
Then if there was a need to make a change, there was already a space to do it.

And as for the placement, I wanted to make sure so I asked an employee who worked in the Publicity Department creating Key Sets. I was told that it was placed where they had more room. There was NO reason other than that.

Before we move on to the studios, let's look at one last area of concern that involves re-makes of films using different actors BUT the SAME codes. Warner Brothers was one of the worse to do this. Numerous times Warner Brothers would re-make a film 5 to 10 years later and then use the same production code for BOTH films.

For example, *Two Against the World* was released in 1932 starring Constance Bennett with the working title of *Higher Ups*. In 1936, Warner Brothers released *Two Against the World* starring Humphrey Bogart.

It was also released under the TV title *One Fatal Hour* and the British title *Case of Mrs. Pembroke*. BOTH the 1932 and the 1936 films used the SAME CODE.

For this reason, when possible, always try to reconfirm the identification by a second source. Once you identify a still by the production code, if there are actors in the still, try to confirm their identity.

If you are a veteran at production stills, then you know that you will run into every scenario imaginable. You basically have to be a detective looking for clues to the identity of THAT still. So any information that can be gleaned from the still, such as distributors, markings on the back, scene explanations, magazine stamps, etc., are potential clues.

~~~~~~~~~~

CINEMA RETRO

BRINGING CINEMA OF THE PAST INTO THE FUTURE IN A NEW MAGAZINE DEVOTED TO 60'S & 70'S

http://www.cinemaretro.com

CINEMA RETRO
PO Box 1570
Christchurch
Dorset BH23 4XS England
Tel: + 44 (0) 870 4423 007
Fax: + 44 (0) 1425 273068
solopublishing@firenet.uk.com

USA OFFICE:
PO Box 152
Dunellen, NJ 08812
USA
Tel: + 001 732 752 7257
Fax: + 001 732 752 6959
cinemaretro@hotmail.com

kinoart.net

ORIGINAL MOVIE POSTERS AND LOBBY CARDS

12,000 SELECTED VINTAGE INTERNATIONAL POSTERS AVAILABLE

WOLFGANG JAHN
SULZBURGSTR. 126
50937 COLOGNE
GERMANY
+49 221 1698728

CHAPTER 9

INDIVIDUAL STUDIOS

Before we start with the individual studios, let's cover one additional situation. It didn't really belong in the last chapter because it is more of a research problem. But it is one that should be addressed.

Many of the major studios submitted their primary production code numbers to the Library of Congress. These records are a tremendous help with one caveat. Almost all of the production codes submitted **DID NOT INCLUDE THE LETTER PREFIX THAT WAS ASSIGNED BY SOME OF THE INDIVIDUAL STUDIOS.**

So, while the production code number would be the same, only some have letter prefixes. In several instances, there are different letter prefixes.

The bottom line is that numbers recorded at the Library of Congress may require additional research.

Columbia Pictures

Columbia's production codes are by far the most confusing and most difficult to use for identification. This may be an indication that Columbia was not quite certain how to effectively number and utilize production codes.

Columbia started production codes for their 1926-1927 season. The first film to have codes was *False Alarm*, which was issued a "C-1" production code.

They produced 24 films that season, marking them "C-1" through "C-24." The Library of Congress records show only the numbers 1-24, but the stills reflect the letter "C," a dash (-) and the number.

The next season (1927-1928), they produced 30 films, with the first one being *The Blood Ship*. Instead of issuing new production codes, they simply started over with their numbering, marking them "C-1" through "C-30."

The next season (1928-1929), they produced 31 films, starting with *Court Martial*. Again, they simply started their numbering system over, marking them "C-1" through "C-31."

Columbia repeated this production code numbering pattern for the first eleven years of film production. In other words, Columbia has 11 different C-1's, 11 different C-2's, 11 different C-3's, etc.

In addition, Columbia numbered their codes based on filming seasons and not by calendar years, compounding the problems with identification.

For example, "C-7" in the 1929-1930 season was *The Melody Man*, while "C-7" in the 1930-1931 season was *Madonna of the Streets*. Both of these films were released in 1930, even though they were from two different filming seasons.

Well, it seems that after eleven years, Columbia was getting confused, so they changed their numbering system.

For the twelfth year, Columbia didn't start back over with the number "1." They primarily used "A-COL," dash (-) and then the number. But some of the stills continue to show a "C-number" also.

For the thirteenth year (1935-1936 season), Columbia used "B-COL" as the primary prefix, but some of the stills continue to show a "C-number" also.

For the fourteenth year (1936-1937 season), Columbia used "C-COL" as their primary prefix.

From 1937 to 1943, Columbia used a "D-COL" prefix.

From 1943 to 1956 they changed to just a "D-(number)", and starting in 1957 they changed to using "CPC" as the prefix.

BUT, during that entire time, some stills continued to show just a "C-number" also.

In addition, Columbia would sometimes mark individual stills within one title's set two or three different ways.

For portrait codes, Columbia usually wrote the celebrity name's out in full.

In the example on the next page, the portrait still of Leslie Brooks has her name written in the bottom left corner.

Educational Pictures

Educational Pictures was started in 1919 by Earle (E. W.) Hammons. While Hammons did distribute some educational and travelogue films, they primarily distributed comedy shorts.

Educational started using production codes in 1920. Their codes consisted of four numbers. This marking procedure stayed consistent through the years except for 1932.

In 1932, Education changed their production code numbering by adding "32" (representing the year). This addition resulted in a six-digit production code number. The following year, Education went back to using just four digits for their production code.

In 1938, Hammons tried to move into feature film production by starting Grand National Pictures. Unfortunately, this venture was a financial disaster which ultimately bankrupted both companies. The Educational-produced shorts were sold off to Astor in 1940.

We have no portrait codes recorded for Educational Pictures.

Fox Film To 20th Century Fox

Fox Film started in 1915, but our first recording of Fox production codes began in 1917.

Fox utilized a "letter dash (-) number" production code. As they increased production, they quite often had the director use his initials or an abbreviation and then numbers.

Fox maintained this letter- number tradition until their merger in 1935.

20th Century utilized a "XXC-number," which was usually four digits. The last two digits were "00."

When sound was introduced into the industry, only Warner Bros. and Fox Film were ready with the necessary equipment to produce films with sound. Fox had been producing sound newsreels so they were prepared for the conversion to sound. Fox immediately became one of the largest film producers in the country.

In 1929, Fox was poised to purchase MGM, but William Fox was in a very bad car accident. While he was in the hospital, the stock market crash of 1929 basically bankrupted him. He was ousted in 1930 and Fox Film was sold.

After the merger in 1935, the 20th Century Fox production code system changed to primarily a number system with an occasional letter-number code.

Fox Film portrait codes either carried an "FX-number" or more commonly the celebrity's initials. This can be seen on the Carol Lombard portrait still on the next page. Note the "CL7" code on the bottom right of the still. "CL" represents Carol Lombard and 7 is the still number.

Starting right after the merger in 1935, 20th Century Fox portrait codes primarily had an "F- number." The still below of Marilyn Monroe is marked "F-999."

This continued until the late 1950s and then it was changed to a "G-number."

Metro Goldwyn Mayer

Goldwyn Pictures was formed in 1916 by Samuel Goldfish (who changed his name to Goldwyn). In 1917, Goldwyn started using production codes. They used an all number system and started with the number "1," which was for the film *Fields of Honor*. They continued consecutively until the merger.

Metro Pictures started out in 1915 distributing films produced by Solax, the first female owned movie studio. The woman was Alice Guy-Blache who created the first story films in France in 1896.

The first production codes that we have on file for Metro was in 1921. They used number codes and letter codes, sometimes different codes for the same film. Their production codes were that way until their merger in 1925.

MGM production codes started in 1925, of course. Because of their diversity, they used every different kind of code - some just letters, some just numbers, and some letter/number combinations. MGM heavily used portrait codes for about everything.

In the 1920s and early 1930s, the most common way MGM marked their portraits was with the celebrity name written out in full along with their initials. See an example of this on the Buster Keaton portrait still on the next page. The initials "BK" are for Buster Keaton.

They were known for the MG series and MGMP series which had the celebrity name written out, and a 4, 5, or 6 digit number afterwards, as seen on the Hedda Hopper portrait still on the next page.

Sometime it would be the MG or MGMP series with the number but without the celebrity name. Sometimes the prefix letters were an LM or an E.

Many celebrities had numerous portrait codes, and some even blocks of codes.

For example, we have recorded 33 different MGM portrait codes just for Anne Francis.

Paramount Pictures

Paramount was BY FAR the most aggressive studio. Paramount was probably the studio that initially created the production code system.

The first production codes we have on file start in 1912, the earliest production codes that we have found. This was actually two years prior to officially becoming Paramount.

Paramount continuously pushed the envelope with new innovations, such as their routing cards, their streamlining of the production process and even their control boards for directors. They were also the most aggressive with copyrights and distribution.

In the early years, they utilized a simple number system. By the early 1920s, Paramount had both an east coast and west coast production office. They had a very confusing dual system with each office creating their own production codes.

Their California offices used an "L" Series code while their New York office used the code "NYKN" (New York Key Numbers). Quite often a title would be presented in BOTH series types with different numbers assigned.

Here's a clip from the original Paramount list:

PROD.#	DESC	TITLE	DIRECTOR	STAR	YR
460	L SERIES	DRUMS OF FATE	MAIGNE	M. MINTER	1923
460	NYKN	BACK HOME AND BROKE (SEE F-245)	GREEN	T. MEIGHAN	1922
461	L SERIES	ADAM'S RIB	DEMILLE	M. SILLS	1923
462	L SERIES	WHITE FLOWER	IVERS	B. COMPSON	1923
463	L SERIES	COVERED WAGON	CRUZE	J. KERRIGAN	1923
464	L SERIES	BELLA DONNA	FITZMAURICE	P. NEGRI	1923
464	NYKN	NICE PEOPLE	DEMILLE	W. REID	1922
465	L SERIES	NOBODY'S MONEY	WORLSEY	J. HOLT	1923
466	L SERIES	RACING HEARTS	POWELL	A. AYRES	1923
466	NYKN	SIREN CALL	WILLAT	D. DALTON	1922
467	L SERIES, NYKN	BORDERLAND		A. AYRES	1922
468	L SERIES	TIGER'S CLAW (SEE # 514)	HENABERY	J. HOLT	1923
468	NYKN	MAN UNCONQUERABLE	HENABERY	J. HOLT	1922
469	L SERIES	PRODIGAL DAUGHTERS	WOOD	G. SWANSON	1923
469	NYKN	TO HAVE AND TO HOLD	FITZMAURICE	B. COMPSON	1922
470	L SERIES	TRAIL OF THE LONESOME PINE	MAIGNE	M. MINTER	1923
470	NYKN	OLD HOMESTEAD	CRUZE	BARNES	1922

The list of letter prefixes, which was a lot smaller, had an additional code that identified smaller groups, such as Artcraft, Hal Wallis, and Pine Thomas.

Paramount portrait codes almost always have a "P" in front of a three or four digit number, as seen on the Martha Raye still on the next page.

Paramount normally did not issue all the multiple codes except for when someone left the company and then came back later. Usually a new code would be assigned.

Be careful not to confuse Paramount portrait codes with Republic movie codes which sometimes also used a "P-number."

MARTHA RAYE in PARAMOUNT PICTURES

Pathe Exchange

Pathe Exchange was formed in 1914 as the U. S. distribution arm of France's Pathe-Freres. The first production codes we have on record for Pathe were Hal Roach codes used on the Lonesome Luke series in 1915. They continued as the primary distributor for Hal Roach shorts.

Pathe separated from Pathe-Freres in 1921 and was purchased by Merrill Lynch. It was later acquired by Joseph Kennedy. Outside of Hal Roach codes, they primarily used all number codes. Pathe portrait codes were the celebrity initials.

Republic Pictures

Republic Pictures started using production codes in 1935, when they first went into production. Republic, like Paramount, normally had two different numbers for the same film. This might be due to the fact that Republic distributed films for smaller production companies and then re-marked the stills with their own distribution numbers. But it continued throughout their productions.

Republic does have the distinction of being the ONLY studio that normally placed a **separate number for their REISSUES**. Republic portrait codes were the celebrity's initials.

RKO

RKO was formed in 1928 and immediately started using production codes. Generally they utilized two different codes for the same title. One was a letter code which was quite often the initials for the film. The other was a number code. By the late 1930s, their system changed to be all letters or letter-number combinations. This continued for the remainder of their existence.

RKO portrait codes were the celebrity's initials as seen on the Shelley Winters still above. Note the letters "SW" for <u>S</u>helly <u>W</u>inters.

United Artists

United Artists was formed in 1919 and immediately utilized production codes. UA production codes were normally letter codes or letter-number codes. Rarely is there just a number code.

United Artists portrait codes primarily used the celebrity initials as seen in the Jane Russell portrait on the preceding page. They also had an additional letter-number system that was used for some portraits.

Universal Studios

Universal Studios was founded in 1912. By 1914, Universal was using production codes on its stills.

Universal primarily used numbers with an occasional letter code or letter-number code.

When we initially started researching production codes, we acquired an official list of Universal Studios production codes. The list was great and even included production code numbers that were NOT used and left dormant.

One problem that we had with the official Universal list was that when the film title was changed after leaving production, the official list did not correct the title. That resulted in a larger than normal number of working titles.

We have marked all the working titles in our *Movie Still Identification Book* and online in our member section of www.MovieStillID.com.

Universal portrait codes were the celebrity initials as seen in the Kay Francis portrait still seen on the next page. Note the "KF" in the lower left corner.

Warner Bros.

Warner Bros. started producing features in 1918, and by 1919 were using production codes.

The early WB production codes were all over the place. They utilized number codes, letter codes, letter-number codes, etc. This continued to the conversion to sound. At that time they started moving to all letter codes.

This trend continued to the late 1940s when they moved again to using all number codes with an occasional letter or letter-number code.

First National and Warner Bros. portrait codes became the celebrity initials as seen on this Patricia Ellis portrait still on the next page. Note the code "PE" on the bottom right.

Additional Portrait Information

Here are some additional portrait markings that might help.

A lot of smaller distributors used initials for their portrait shots. This included: British Gaumont; Goldwyn; Grand National; Metro; Monogram; Realart (1910s-1920s); Robertson Cole; Selznick; and Tiffany.

Vitagraph used VX-number. Metro sometimes used MPX-number. Realart (1910s-1920s) sometimes used RPC-number.

Here are some oddities to look out for when dealing with portrait codes:

Some studios would combine the portrait code with another code such as "F" for Fashion or "P" for Publicity. The additional code could precede or follow the portrait code.

An example would be "ILF" might be a fashion shot of Ida Lupino, or "PRR" might be a publicity shot of Robert Ryan.

Other common codes are:

> "FGP" - Fox General Publicity
> "F" - Fashion
> "F" - Feature
> "OSP" - Off Set Publicity

Finally, there are some definite exceptions. Here are a few:

A. The portrait code letters sometimes refer to a celebrity's real name, before the studio changed it. Examples include: "AC" - Anthony (Tony) Curtis; "BA" - Burnu Acquanetta; and "MMac" - Martha MacVicar, better known as Martha Vickers.

B. Warner Bros in particular played with the standard initial pattern. Joan Blondell is not "JB" but "BL"; Dolores Del Rio is not "DDR" but "RIO; instead of RR, Rosalind Russell is ROS"; Basil Rathbone is not "BR" but "RATH"; and Alexis Smith is not "AS" but "LEX."

C. Some codes refer to duos or groups: "AC" - Abbott & Costello; "AS" - the Andrews Sisters; "CSB" - Crime School Boys; and "FMM" - Fibber McGee & Molly.

D. And then there's MGM. While Warner Bros was satisfied to let "JC" stand for Jack Carson, James Cagney, James Craig, Jeanne Cagney and Joseph Cotton, simultaneously, MGM used an "X" or "2" to distinguish Jean Harlow ("JHX") from Jean Hersholt ("JH"); Judy Garland ("JGXX") from John Gilbert ("JG"); and Greer Garson ("GXGX") from Gladys George ("GXG") from Greta Garbo ("GGX").

~~~~~~~~~~

channingposters

ORIGINAL
MOVIE POSTERS,
LOBBY CARDS, AND
AUTOGRAPHED ITEMS

**CHANNING THOMSON
P. O. BOX 330232
SAN FRANCISCO, CA 94133-0232**

Email: channinglylethomson@att.net
ebay: http://stores.ebay.com/CHANNINGPOSTERS

SIMON DWYER!

GENUINE VINTAGE MOVIE POSTERS
DATING FROM THE 1920's
TO THE 1970'S BROUGHT
FROM CINEMA HOARDINGS
AROUND THE WORLD TO
YOUR FRONT DOOR

Simon Dwyer
7 Epirus Mews
London SW6 7UP
United Kingdom

www.SimonDwyer.com
SIMON.DWYER@LAKESVILLE.COM

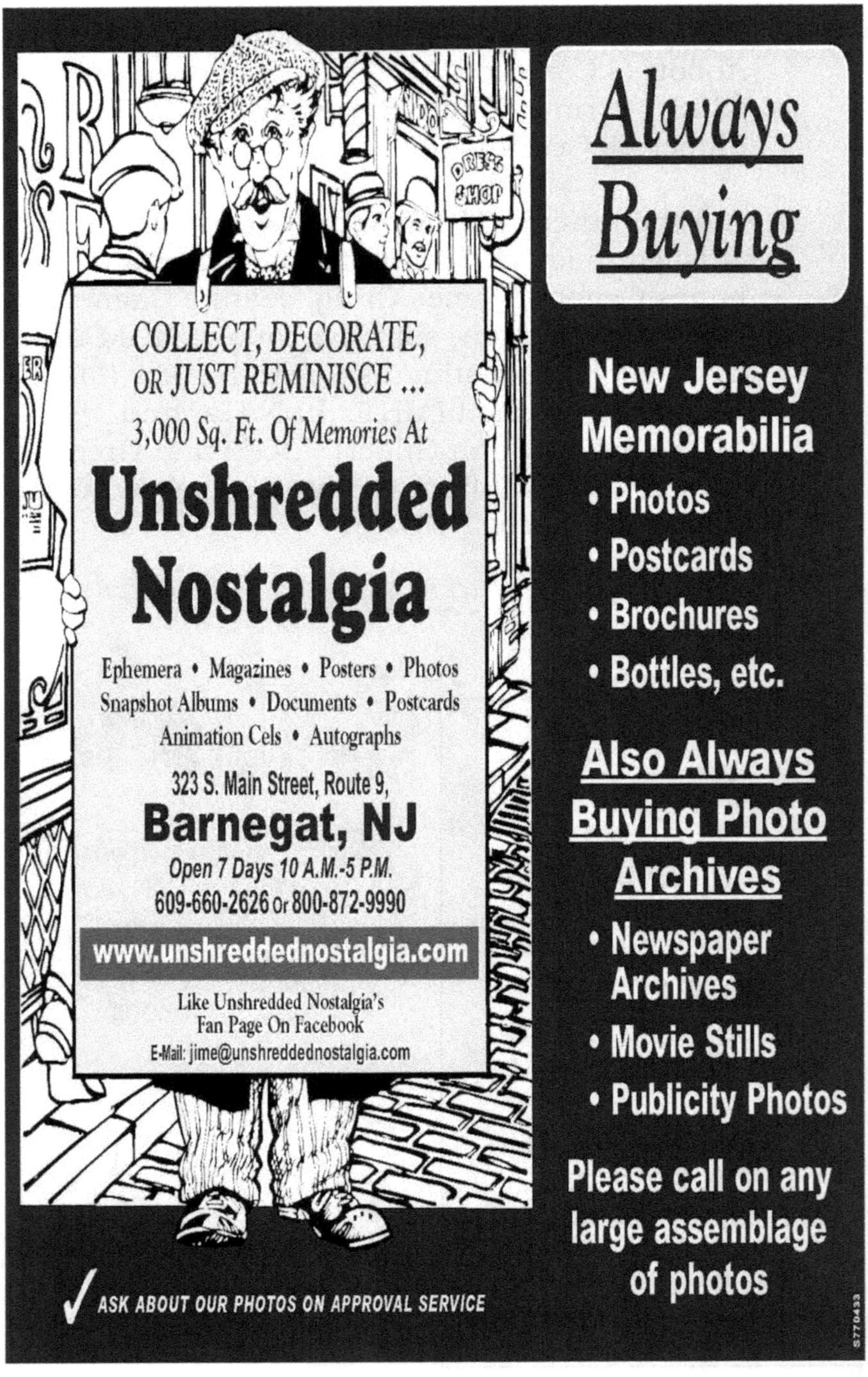
COLLECT, DECORATE,
OR JUST REMINISCE ...
3,000 Sq. Ft. Of Memories At
Unshredded
Nostalgia
Ephemera • Magazines • Posters • Photos
Snapshot Albums • Documents • Postcards
Animation Cels • Autographs
323 S. Main Street, Route 9,
Barnegat, NJ
Open 7 Days 10 A.M.-5 P.M.
609-660-2626 Or 800-872-9990
www.unshreddednostalgia.com
Like Unshredded Nostalgia's
Fan Page On Facebook
E-Mail: jime@unshreddednostalgia.com
ASK ABOUT OUR PHOTOS ON APPROVAL SERVICE
Always
Buying
New Jersey
Memorabilia
• Photos
• Postcards
• Brochures
• Bottles, etc.
Also Always
Buying Photo
Archives
• Newspaper
Archives
• Movie Stills
• Publicity Photos
Please call on any
large assemblage
of photos

CHAPTER 10

TOOLS FOR IDENTIFYING UNKNOWN MOVIE STILLS

While the research and preparation of this book was MASSIVE, we understand that there is an unbelievable amount of work that still needs documenting in this area.

We've tried our best to present the most accurate and reliable information possible, and hope this will be beneficial to you in your research.

We realize that knowing what production codes are and how to identify them is just the first step. NOW, you need the codes to help you identify that unknown still.

We have two tools to help you with that problem:

(1) *Movie Still Identification Book*; and

(2) The Website www.MovieStillID.com.

Movie Still Identification Book

The first tool is the 2013 Edition of our *Movie Still Identification Book*. This 5th edition has 45,400 codes to help you with your identification problems. We have tried to make the process as simple as possible.

Here are the instructions to show you how easy it is to use our Movie Still Identification Book.

For this edition, we wanted to help you identify your still. So you simply:

Get your code;

Look it up in the appropriate code log;

See who used that particular code – PERIOD.

Before we break down the columns, there are TWO (2) sections: Letters and Numbers. If the production code on the unidentified still STARTS with a letter, go to the Letter Section. If the code STARTS with a number, go to the Numbers Section.

You will see the same five columns in each section:

1. Code
2. Title/Name
3. Director/Type
4. Studio/Distributor
5. Year

Let's take a look at each column.

Code

The code refers to the letter/number code etched on the still that you are trying to identify. We have production codes, portrait codes, series codes, and studio codes. All are together and in either alphabetical - alpha/numeric order (in the Letters Section) or numeric - numeric/alpha order (in the Numbers Section), There are some numbers that start with zero ("0") which comes before 1.

Title/Name

This column has the film title, personality name or studio name. But there are several additional codes included in the column.

 a. Major aka's are in parenthesis beside the title.

 b. For a major release from a different country, the country code is included, i.e. ("IT") Italy; ("UK") United Kingdom; ("FR") France; ("GER") Germany; ("JAP") Japan; ("SP") Spain, etc.

 c. Animation – ("t") We marked as many as we could during editing.

 d. Shorts – ("sh") - We marked as many as we could during editing.

 e, Original year – when a reissue had a different number, we put the original year by the title.

 f. Working titles have an (*) asterisk at the end of the title

Director/Type

The primary director is listed in all capital letters. When it is a portrait, series or studio code, they are shown in small letters.

Studio/Distributor

The major distributor is listed (NOT the production company) for production codes. For portrait, series or studio codes, we tried to list the major studio when available.

Year

Year of release is shown for production codes. When it is a reissue, the year is shown as "R" plus a 2 digit reissue year. Some series and portrait codes have ranges shown.

THAT'S IT – SIMPLIFY!!

Movie Still ID Website

The book is very easy to use, but if you need more, there's the website www.MovieStillID.com.

The first advance website dedicated to research and documentation of movie stills. Our 2013 edition *Movie Still Identification Book* has 45,400 codes to help identify unknown movie, series, portrait, serial and TV stills. Our *Movie Still Archive* is now open over 300 galleries and 20,000 images. Take a look. And finally, our advance *Research* area is a member only area and includes access to our new 2013 edition plus sorts by Director and Studio and loads of additional research.

2013 Movie Still Identification Book and Production Code Basics

Movie Stills Archive

Advance Still Research Member Area

A yearly membership in the website costs the same as the book. In addition to the 45,400 codes that are available in the book, we have room to sort the information and present the codes in different ways. For example, we have the production codes sorted by over 2000 directors in case you are doing research on directors.

We also have the production codes sorted by studios, so if you are researching Mack Sennett, Hal Roach, Educational Picture shorts, or whatever studio, we have it available.

And finally, we post New Additions, which are production codes that we have acquired since the compilation of the 2013 Edition.

We will continue to document and expand in all directions on our websites.

Be sure to visit our website (MovieStillID.com) to see our Movie Still Archive.

Other Research Websites

For movie poster information, visit our website designed for Beginner to Intermediate collectors (www.LearnAboutMoviePosters.com).

For our exclusive movie poster research database to document, sort and research all types of movie posters, visit our website :

(www.MoviePosterDataBase.com).

For advance research for movie poster artists, printers and lithographers logs, lithography plate numbers, studio logos and dating, printers unions, National Screen Service logs and information, and much more, visit our advance website (www.GlobalCinemaResearch.org)

And finally, for our local website on Louisiana Film History, visit our Louisiana website (HollywoodOnTheBayou.com)

Please email (edp@LearnAboutMoviePosters.com) or call (504-298-LAMP) as we would love to show you through our advanced research areas.

We hope that you will enjoy our book. Please let us know your comments and suggestions. Thank you and good luck with your research

Ed and Susan Poole
Film Accessory Researchers

583 Pacific Street - Stanford CT 06902
203.324.9750
www.posterconservation.com

Before — After

LINEN BACKING AND RESTORATION SERVICES

Movie Posters ~ Music Posters
TV Posters ~ Celebrity Posters
Star Wars & James Bond
Harry Potter

Collectormania
17892 Cottonwood Dr
Parker, CO 80134

1-866-630-1648

questions@posterplanet.net
posterplanetfile@aol.com

There are 25,000 posters databased and available at www.movieart.com. Inquire to posters@moviewart.com. We sell posters to collectors, designers and institutions worldwide. Our staff is friendly. We answer questions.

Selling posters since 1979.

IVPDA
international vintage
P O S T E R
dealers association

KIRBY MCDANIEL
MOVIEART

FILM/ART
Original Film Posters

Hollywood, CA

323.363.2969

filmartgallery.com

SPOTLIGHTDISPLAYS.COM

LAMP SPONSORS ADS

Page No.

Amazing 3rd Planet	86
Bags Unlimited	10, 104
Bonhams	63
Channing Lyle Thomson	62, 127
Cinema Retro	103
Conway's Vintage Treasures	85
Dominique Besson	56
eMovieposter.com	9, 104
Ewbanks Auctions	18
Femme, Fatales & Fantasies	85
Film Art Gallery	73, 136
Four Color Comics	55
French Movie Posters	33
Heritage Auctions	34, Back Cover
Hollywood Poster Frames	10, 62
Illustration Gallery	63
Intemporel	85
Kinoart.net	33, 103
L'Imagerie Gallery	18, 86
Last Moving Picture Show	85
Limited Runs	55
Movie Poster Bid	137
Movie Poster Exchange	17
Movie Art of Austin	33, 136
Movie Art Gmbh	55
Original Poster	74
Past Posters	55
Poster Conservation	135
Posteropolis	73
Poster Planet	62, 136
Robert Edwards Auction	64
Simon Dwyer	127
Spotlight Displays	73, 136
The Cinema Trade	84
Unshredded Nostalgia	128
Vintage Movie Memorabilia	73
Yazoo Mills	74

www.ingramcontent.com/pod-product-compliance
Lightning Source LLC
Chambersburg PA
CBHW070810100426
42742CB00012B/2322